Entertaining St

Entertaining Strangers was first p[...]
1985 by the people of Dorchester [...]
premièred at the National Theatre, London, in October 1987 with
Judi Dench as Sarah Eldridge and Tim Pigott-Smith as Henry
Moule. The production was directed by Peter Hall.

'This is English left-wing social drama at its sturdiest and finest:
humane, argumentative, utterly unafraid of human realities, and
seething with indignation and compassion.'

John Peter, *Sunday Times*

'Generous, sprawling and highly enjoyable . . . Moule, the detested
scourge of the impious becomes the beloved champion of the poor
. . . the painful stirring of his compassion becomes the most
dramatic element of the play.'

Michael Ratcliffe, *Observer*

DAVID EDGAR

David Edgar was born in 1948 in Birmingham. His stage work –
some forty plays in all – includes *Excuses Excuses* (1972); *Dick
Deterred* (1974); *Saigon Rose* (1976); *Mary Barnes* (1978);
Teendreams (with Susan Todd, 1979) and *That Summer* (1987). He
has written four plays for the Royal Shakespeare Company, for
whom he acts as literary adviser: they are *Destiny* (1976); *The Jail
Diary of Albie Sachs* (1978); *Nicholas Nickleby* (1980); and *Maydays*
(1983). He received the John Whiting award for *Nicholas Nickleby*
(which also won him a Tony award in New York), and the *Plays
and Players* best play award for *Maydays*. His television work
includes adaptations of *Destiny*, *Jail Diary* and *Nicholas Nickleby*,
and his first film, *Lady Jane*, was released in 1986.

Front cover: Tim Pigott-Smith as the Reverend Henry Moule,
*National Theatre, London, 1987. (Photograph: John Haynes). Back
cover: David Edgar by Doug Pratt.*

by the same author

BALL BOYS (Pluto Press)
ENTERTAINING STRANGERS (*the Dorchester version*)
DESTINY
DICK DETERRED (Monthly Review Press, New York)
MARY BARNES
MAYDAYS
NICHOLAS NICKLEBY (Dramatists' Play Service, New York)
TEENDREAMS and OUR OWN PEOPLE
WRECKERS
PLAYS: ONE
(Destiny, Mary Barnes, The Jail Diary of Albie Sachs, Saigon
Rose, O Fair Jerusalem)

DAVID EDGAR

Entertaining Strangers

a new version of
*Entertaining Strangers: A Play for
Dorchester*

A Methuen Paperback

A METHUEN MODERN PLAY

First published in Great Britain in the Methuen New Theatrescript
series in 1986 by Methuen London Ltd, 11 New Fetter Lane,
London EC4P 4EE and in the United States of America by
Methuen Inc, 29 West 35th Street, New York NY 10001.
Revised and entirely re-set in 1988 for the Methuen Modern
Plays series.
Copyright © 1986, 1988 by David Edgar

Set in Plantin by 🕏 Tek Art Ltd, Croydon, Surrey
Printed in Great Britain by
Richard Clay Ltd, Bungay, Suffolk

British Library Cataloguing in Publication Data

Edgar, David
   Entertaining strangers. – 2nd ed. –
   (A Methuen modern play).
   I. Title
   822'.914   PR6055.D44

   ISBN 0-413-16670-8

To Nancy

Introduction

I first saw Dorchester driving through it towards Lyme Regis, where Ann Jellicoe's community play *The Western Women* was being performed, with a cast of 150+, to a packed, promenading audience in the local secondary school. I'd known about Ann Jellicoe's pioneering work in large-scale community drama, but was unprepared for its overwhelming impact in practice. The following morning, I was asked to consider being the writer for her next-but-one project – a play for Dorchester, the Dorset county town. It was an offer I could not decently refuse.

Although built round a 'core' of professionals (director, writer, stage manager, composer, designer), Ann Jellicoe's productions arise out of the resources, interests and needs of the community for and by which they're created. I quickly discovered that Dorchester is blessed with a large number of local historians, and virtually the first thing I did was set up a group of researchers on whose diligent and imaginative labours much of the play is based. I also discovered that the town was definitely not interested in my writing about any of its three main claims to fame, and perhaps reasonably felt it needed a play about the bloody assizes, the Tolpuddle martyrs and/or Thomas Hardy like a hole in the head.

In fact, the story we eventually hit upon did get in a little Hardy by the back door. The Reverend Henry Moule of Fordington (Dorchester's slum suburb) is clearly the original of Angel Clare's fundamentalist father in *Tess of the D'Urbevilles*, and elements of his story crop up in *Under the Greenwood Tree* and the short story *A Changed Man* (in which Henry Moule's story is conflated with that of Augustus Handley, the born-again dragoon). Further, Henry's son Horace was one of Hardy's greatest friends, and the tragic climax of Horace's life is the subject of several Hardy poems and clearly a partial inspiration for *Jude the Obscure*.

The other half of the story – that of Sarah Eldridge, founder of Dorchester's leading brewery – is less well documented. Indeed, it was the result of a considerable degree of historical detective work by the research group, who patiently culled scrapbook, microfilm, ledger and in several cases gravestone for pieces of a largely-lost family story.

In 1985, it felt right to be doing a play which confronted the values of entrepreneurial zeal with those of religious fundamentalism. Such a confrontation is perhaps even more apposite now. Much of the first half of the play is set in the 1830s – the decade in which the mighty industrial revolution which had been brewing for 50 years finally flapped its great iron wings and flew, promising a seemingly limitless progress towards economic and social emancipation. But then the story moves to the 1850s, a decade in which the confines of that revolution became painfully apparent. For all the technological achievement of the first half of the nineteenth century, by the advent of the second great cholera epidemic the Victorians knew little more about the workings of their own bodies than the Tudors. And in cholera they faced a hitherto unknown disease, whose means of spread was a mystery and which attacked the new classes in the expanding towns to a disproportionate and often devastating extent. Nor surprisingly, the decade saw the upsurge of a number of movements that sought to address themselves to the crisis in the towns, from the utopian Christian Socialism of F.D. Maurice and Thomas Hughes to those preventive health campaigns which correctly identified the cure of cholera not in moral but in sanitary reform.

Like all of Ann Jellicoe's plays, *Entertaining Strangers* took the best part of two years to put together, and involved not only a cast of 180 (ranging in age from 3 to 85) but also a gargantuan army of painters, carpenters, costume- and prop-makers, musicians, accountants, caterers, babysitters, drivers, publicists, printers, box-office helpers and ushers throughout the town and beyond. In reworking the play for the more modest resources on offer at the National Theatre, I've been able to develop and I think deepen the relationships of the central characters, and I've allowed myself considerably greater leeway with their history. But I realised early on that I would need to create some kind of metaphorical surrogate for the sheer power of Dorchester's numbers (and the emotional strength of the fact that the play was performed in a church established by one of the central characters, within a stone's throw of a brewery founded by the other).

In outline, *Entertaining Strangers* is about the attempt to impose two eminently Victorian values on an English county town in the process of transformation from an essentially rural to an urban society. Both sets of beliefs are found wanting, in face of the older and more basic realities which emerge to challenge them during the course of the play. These realities – and the ancient mysteries that both acknowledge and confront them – are represented in the new version by fragments from a mummers' play, which is sometimes actually happening, but more often takes the form of a snatch or echo in the mind. The mummers' play itself is a compound of many, drawn from various styles and forms of the old art. But, as has always been true, the play is acted by performers with hidden faces, with a seriousness, if not a solemnity, appropriate to its ancient significance.

David Edgar

Entertaining Strangers was first performed on 18 November 1985, in St Mary's Church, Dorchester, as a community play presented in association with the Colway Theatre Trust, and directed by Ann Jellicoe.

This revised version of the play was first performed in the Cottesloe auditorium of the National Theatre on 9 October 1987, with the following cast:

THE ELDRIDGE HOUSEHOLD

SARAH ELDRIDGE	Judi Dench
CHARLES ELDRIDGE	Michael Byrne
SOPHIE	Charlotte Coleman
EMILY	Helen Fitzgerald
CHARLES JNR	Nicholas Simpson/ Corin Helliwell
SARAH ALBINIA	Nadia Chambers
CHRISTIAN, maid	Sally Dexter
FANNY LOCK, maid	Shirley Henderson
JOHN JAMES BESANT	Michael Bottle
JOHN TIZARD	Peter Woodward

THE MOULE HOUSEHOLD

HENRY MOULE	Tim Pigott-Smith
MARY MOULE	Janet Whiteside
GEORGE	Patrick Brennan
HORACE	Garry Cooper
CHARLES	Simon Scott
HANDLEY JNR	Steven Mackintosh
HENRY JNR	Nicholas Simpson/ Corin Helliwell
GEORGE as a child	James Hillier Brook/ Ian Harris
ELLEN WRIGHT, nurse	Frances Quinn
HANNAH, maid	Joanne Lamb

COURT AND GENTRY

CAPT WILLIAM HENNING	John Bluthal
ANN HENNING	Sally Dexter
MARY FRAMPTON	Mary McLeod
HENRY FRAMPTON	Robert Arnold
ROBERT WILLIAMS	Basil Henson
LIEUTENANT VANDALEUR	Michael Bottle

PROFESSIONAL

THOMAS PATCH	Patrick Brennan
GEORGE ANDREWS	Michael Bottle
DR CHRISTOPHER ARDEN	Basil Henson

TRADE

JAMES BROOKS	Peter Gordon
ANN BESANT	Jenny Galloway
ALFRED MASON	Robert Arnold
GEORGE LODER	Richard Bonneville
JOHN GALPIN	Peter Gordon

LABOURING/AGRICULTURAL

JOHN LOCK	Richard Bonneville
MARTHA LOCK	Jenny Galloway
LOUISA	Laura McMahon/ Annabelle Ryan
JANE WHITING	Mary McLeod
MARTHA	Nadia Chambers
FIRST COMMUNICANT	Simon Scott
SECOND COMMUNICANT	Michael Bottle
THIRD COMMUNICANT	Garry Cooper
WILLIAM BARTLETT	John Bluthal
WILLIAM FUDGE	Robert Arnold
EDWARD FUDGE	Steven Mackintosh
NATTY SEALE	Basil Henson
JANE SIBLEY	Helen Fitzgerald
LIZZIE SIBLEY	Charlotte Coleman
ALBERT	James Hillier Brook/ Ian Harris

FLORENCE CHAFFLEY, child	Joanne Lamb
FLORENCE CHAFFLEY	Frances Quinn
BENJAMIN VOSS	Robert Arnold
SARAH HOLLAND	Frances Quinn

OUTSIDERS

CAPT AUGUSTUS HANDLEY	Peter Woodward
SERGEANT	Richard Bonneville
MR MACARTE	John Bluthal
MR HENGLER	Peter Woodward
MR TURNLEY	Simon Scott
YOUNG WARDER	Patrick Brennan

Mummers, congregations, race-goers, cholera victims, crowds and other parts were played by members of the company.

Directed by Peter Hall
Designed by William Dudley
Lighting by Gerry Jenkinson
Music by Dominic Muldowney
Director of the Mellstock Band David Townsend

Entertaining Strangers is based on original research by Bridget Bowen, Beth Brooke, Billie Brown, Terry Hearing, Joan Kimber and Jill Pope. Alan Chedzoy was dialect consultant for both versions.

ACT ONE

Scene One

1.1.1. **The Mummers' Play: The Presentation.** *The characters are the* PRESENTER, FATHER CHRISTMAS, *the* DRAGON *and* ST GEORGE. *Rhythmic knocking punctuates the speeches.*

PRESENTER.

> Make room! Make room for us to sport,
> For in this place we do resort.
> We have not come to laugh or jeer,
> But for a pocketful of money and a skinful of beer.
> And if you believe not what I say:
> Enter old Father Christmas! Clear the Way!

FATHER CHRISTMAS.

> I am Old Father Christmas,
> Welcome or welcome not.
> I hope Old Father Christmas
> Will never be forgot.
> And now if you will our sport to start:
> Come on, bold Dragon, play your part!

DRAGON. Who's he that seeks the Dragon's blood,
> Who calls so angry and so loud?
> With my long teeth and scurvy jaw,
> Of such I'll break up half a score.

But before ST GEORGE *can respond to the challenge, the knocking becomes less rhythmic and more urgent, and focus shifts to:*

1.1.2. **The Green Dragon Inn, Dorchester,** *towards the end of 1829. The room is in near darkness.* SARAH ELDRIDGE, *32, the proprietor, has been roused from bed. She hurries through the room to answer the door.*

SARAH. Charles! Christian! Charles! Do *no one* but I hear the door?

She opens the door. A tall young clergyman stands there. He is HENRY MOULE, *28.*

Why, parson.

MOULE. Madam, I am so sorry.

SARAH. Yes, well –

MOULE. I'm afraid it's very late, but I –

SARAH. What was it you were wan-

MOULE. – but when I saw the light above –

SARAH's servant CHRISTIAN, *still in her teens, hurries on, assembling her person.*

CHRISTIAN. Oh, ma'am, I'm sorry –

SARAH. Christian. Please to see if Sophie's woken, and then find your master.

CHRISTIAN. Yes, ma'am. Yes, directly.

She hurries out.

MOULE. It was – it seemed to be the only light in Dorchester.

SARAH. Well, as you say, 'tis very late. Please to come in.

MOULE *nods a bow and enters.* SARAH *closes the door.*

In fact, the light is in my malthouse. At advent time, my husband lets the mummers practise there. Some folks do say that 'tis next-door to witchcraft, but we don't hold with that.

Slight pause.

Now, parson, I must tell you, that we run a simple alehouse, and it's not our custom to take guests –

Two glove puppets – one a little girl, the other Santa Claus, appear, followed in a few moments by SARAH's *husband* CHARLES, *38. He alternates* 'SOPHIE' *and* 'Santa' *voices.*

CHARLES. 'Santa! Santa!'
'Yes, what is it, Sophie?'

SARAH. What?

CHARLES. 'Santa what's Sarah doing up and round in the middle of the night?' 'Well I don't rightly know old girl, what say we goes and asks her.'

SARAH. *Charles.*

CHARLES. So, what d'you think?

SARAH (*gesturing to* MOULE). I'm sure she'll love them, Charles . . .

CHARLES *turns.*

CHARLES. Oh, I beg your pardon, vicar, I didn't see you there . . .

MOULE (*handing his card to* SARAH). Sir. Ma'am. My name is Henry Moule.

CHARLES *puts out his puppeted hand to shake. He realises, and withdraws.*

I am appointed to I think the adjacent parish to your own. As yet the vicarage is not vacated by my predecessor's widow. And the only inns where I could raise an answer at this hour were full.

SARAH. Well, 'tis market day tomorrow. You should a-been here earlier.

MOULE. I would have been, had my trap not lost a wheel. It took me some time to remount it.

SARAH *looks at* MOULE – *she doesn't expect vicars to be able to change wheels.*

And I appreciate that you do not usually offer accommodation. But as a stranger to your town, I would appreciate it if you could make an exception in this case.

CHRISTIAN *rushes in.*

CHRISTIAN. Now, ma'dam – Miss Sophie's fine, she didn't wake, but I can't find Mr –

SARAH. Now don't fuss, Christian, Mr Eldridge found us by himself.

CHARLES *waggles the puppets at* CHRISTIAN.

Now, could you put the kettle on, and then go make up the settle in the parlour as a bed for Reverend –

She glances at the card. Pronouncing MOULE *'mool'.*

– Moule, then make him up a bottle, for 'tis grown quite brisk and the fire's been dead an hour, while maybe Charles could stable up the parson's animal.

CHARLES. Why, yes, at once, my angel.

He kisses SARAH. *Then, with the puppets, as* 'SOPHIE':

'Say "bye, bye Santa", Sarah.'

SARAH. Oh. Bye bye.

CHRISTIAN *grins and scurries out.* CHARLES *goes too.* SARAH *is embarrassed.*

You will forgive my husband, Mr Moule. He's of a – well, a somewhat expansive cast of character. And we were married just a threemonth since. Now, no doubt your journey's left you tired and thirsty. Would you like a brandy? Or indeed a glass of beer?

MOULE. No, madam, I abstain.

SARAH. Oh, yes, of course. Well, I say 'of course', but 'tis by no means universal. Indeed, there was common talk about your predecessor . . . So, a cup of tea?

MOULE. No, nothing, thank you, ma'am.

A slightly heavy pause.

SARAH ⎱ (*simultaneously*). And so –
MOULE ⎰   In fact –

They gesture each other to continue. SARAH *wins.*

MOULE. In fact, ma'am, it is 'Mole'.

SARAH *looks bemused.*

'Mool' is a mussel.

SARAH. Ah.

Another slightly heavy pause.

MOULE. And so, may *I* enquire –

SARAH. Of course. I'm sorry. Mrs Sarah Eldridge, the Green Dragon Inn.

MOULE. I see. How do you do.

SARAH *nods.*

And may I ask, who is the child?

Slight pause.

SARAH. I beg your pardon?

MOULE. 'Sophie'. If you were married 'but a threemonth since'.

Slight pause.

SARAH (*quite sharply*). Well, Mr Moule, my husband was a widower, left with a small baby. I was a widow, and my first marriage was not fruitful. We met up, and it seemed a most convenient arrangement.

CHARLES *has entered with* MOULE's *bags. He sets them down.*

CHARLES. Well, Mr Moule, you'll guess that 'met up's' not the half of it.

SARAH. Ah, Charles. In fact, it's 'Mole'. 'Mool' is by all accounts a mussel.

CHARLES. You see, afore we met up, I was a domestic steward, to the family of Mr Robert Williams of Little Bredy, of whom you may have heard –

CHRISTIAN *rushes in.*

CHRISTIAN. Bed be made up, ma'am –

SARAH. Well, thank you, Christian –

CHRISTIAN (*to* MOULE). – and the kettle's on –

MOULE. Please, there's no need –

CHARLES. – and Mrs Eldridge, or Mrs Balson, as she was then, called to try and interest me in purchasing her ales and beers, thus saving us the trouble –

SARAH. Charles, I'm sure that Mr Moule –

CHARLES. – and in fact, I was actually raising up a glass of her best brew, to test it like, outside the back door, when master and his guests arrived from riding.

SARAH. *Charles.*

CHARLES. But perhaps 'tis a little late for talespinning.

SARAH. Indeed that's so.

CHARLES. So if the kettle's –

CHRISTIAN. Oh, sir, *no*. (*To* MOULE.) Oh, 'tis the story of the way they met. 'Tis *beautiful*. I never wearies of it.

Pause.

Well, leastwise, while the *kettle* –

SARAH *shrugs.*

CHARLES. So, as I say, the quality arrives, and I'm there, raising up my glass, and as they're passing, Mrs Balson nods, as if to say 'good morning', not disrespectful, like –

CHRISTIAN. – but not *obsequious* –

CHARLES. – indeed, like she don't bow nor scrape nor curtsy. And quite the most superior of all the ladies turns, and whispers –

SARAH. – in the kind of whisper you can hear in Somerset –

CHARLES. To the effect that servants nowadays appear to think that they can stand around –

CHRISTIAN (*correcting*). Can *lounge* around –

CHARLES. – like as if they owned the place. And then, quick as a flash – well she can tell you what she said herself.

He turns to SARAH, *who resists for a moment. But, then:*

SARAH. Well, all I said was, something like, 'Excuse me, madam, but I think you are in error . . . because in fact I'm not in service, I'm in commerce, I'm an independent trading person, ma'am.'

CHRISTIAN. And you should'a seen her *face*.

SARAH (*to* MOULE). She wasn't there.

CHARLES. And then she say –

CHRISTIAN. This is the lady, see –

CHARLES. 'Yes, and I assure you that it's obvious enough what it is you trade in –'

CHRISTIAN (*to* MOULE:) Like, a-smelling of the beer . . .

CHARLES. To which she says:

SARAH. 'Yes, that's right, madam, beer.'

Slight pause.

CHARLES. Go *on*.

SARAH. 'A beverage of malted barley, boiled with hops, fermented with the finest yeast. The pride of Dorsetshire. Retailed as far away as London, at the most select establishments.'

CHARLES (*prompting*). Trafalgar.

SARAH. Yes, 'Chosen to sustain our sailors at the battle of Trafalgar, and throughout the French wars, at Admiral Nelson's personal command.'

CHRISTIAN. His personal, *express* command –

SARAH. 'Yes, that's right. Dorset beer. And may I ask,'

CHRISTIAN. – she asks –

SARAH. 'What *you* do for a living?'

CHARLES, SARAH *and* CHRISTIAN *are vastly amused.* MOULE *is not, which* SARAH *is the first to notice.*

And off they go, and it's really not a very funny story, and I'm sure the parson wants –

CHRISTIAN. Oh, *no.* You're leaving out the best bit, ma'am. 'Cos then he, Mr Eldridge, he do take her hands, that's Mrs Balson's as she was, and say how he never come across a body nothing like what she is and how he do have this little baby who do need a mother, that's like little Sophie, and that's not to mention like his own need of a wife, and thereby and therefore she must wed with him at once, and she, that's Mrs Balson, she do say she could never be like married to a butler, on account of the obsequiousness required, but he that's Mr Eldridge he do say he think that he could be like married to a brewhouse keeper, he do think he has the head for that, and Mrs Balson she do say that she don't plan to be a brewhouse keeper all her life for she has got ambitions like to run a proper brewery or have charge of a coaching inn or something of that character, and that's at *least*, and Mr Eldridge he do say that that's all right with him, and he's about to take things a bit further if you take my drift when he that's Mr Robert Williams hisself, he come back out and he do taste the beer and say that she, that's – her, that she's no cause to feel 'ferior to anybody by way of her business or the product she do sell and may he be the first to wish them every happiness.

(*Pause.*) And so, like – so he was.

Slight pause.

CHARLES. And so he was indeed.

SARAH. Well, yes, that's right, and that be how we met, and since then we've been wed and we do live here in my father's hostelry, we haven't got ourselves a coaching inn but I still live in hope, and that's our story top to tail and I'm convinced the parson don't want nothing better than to be a-bed.

MOULE. That is the case, ma'am.

SARAH. So, Christian, that kettle –

MOULE. But I must say something first.

SARAH. Yes? What?

MOULE. It is, that I have listened to your story with the greatest interest. But I must state nonetheless that I judge your business to be no more than a commerce of corruption, a trade in sin; and that your filial inheritance is gall. Sir, I am sorry to come upon you at this hour, I am most grateful for your hospitality, I need no further service and I would appreciate it if my bill could be prepared for settlement at half past seven at the latest. Goodnight, sir, and ma'am.

MOULE *picks up his bag and goes out.*

Pause.

SARAH. Well. I'll remember that.

CHARLES. He's for St George's? For St George's *Fordington*?

He looks to SARAH *and* CHRISTIAN.

CHRISTIAN. Be better biding here.

1.1.3 **The Mummers' Play:** *The focus shifts to* NARRATORS *below, and, in a moment, to a* MUMMER *aloft.*

NARRATIVE. And thus it was, in 1829, that Henry Moule,

hitherto curate of the church at Gillingham,

proceeded from the Dragon to the adjacent parish of St George's, Fordington,

which, as has often been remarked, embraces Dorchester as an egg enfolds its yolk,

and what was to prove from its first days a most eventful ministry.

The NARRATORS *look up at the* MUMMER *and we look up with them.* ST GEORGE *has his flag, the red cross on a white ground.*

ST GEORGE. I am Saint George, from England sprung,
My name throughout the world has rung.
I'll clip this Dragon's wings, he shall not fly:
I'll cut this wild worm down else I do die.
What mortal man would dare to stand
Afore St George with sword in hand?

Scene Two

1.2.1. **St George's Church, Fordington.** JOHN *and* MARTHA LOCK *(20 and 30) wait by the font, with their baby and* JANE WHITING, *a woman of indeterminate age, status and character. We are not yet aware of it, but the church* ORCHESTRA *is assembling to practise aloft: its members are not in the first flush of youth, and indeed its best friends could not describe its playing as anything other than awful. The clerk,* JAMES BROOKS *appears, as does* HENRY MOULE.

BROOKS. Well, morning to you, Mr Moule.

MOULE. Ah. Mr Brooks.

BROOKS. Now, be you and Mrs Moule well cribbed down in the vicarage?

MOULE. Yes, thank you, Mr Brooks. In fact –

BROOKS. Old parson, he do say, best thing about the parish, you can lumper from the vestry to the vicarage, smoke half a pipe, and be back afore they'm done the Jubilate Deo. Now, what have we this morning. Ah. Baptising little Henry Lock. Good morning John and Martha.

JOHN LOCK. Morning, Mr Brooks.

MARTHA LOCK. Morning, parson.

MOULE. Good morning. And is this . . . a godparent?

BROOKS. Ar. This be Miss Whiting.

JANE WHITING. How'st do.

BROOKS. And we'd a-had her, like, companion as t'other, but he be took bad, and t'will have to be I if that do fay with all the ordinances like.

Pause.

MOULE. Well. Let us proceed. 'Dearly beloved, forasmuch as all men are conceived and born in sin –', um, Mr Clerk?

BROOKS. Sir?

MOULE. There is no water.

BROOKS. Water, sir?

MOULE. No water in the font.

BROOKS *laughs. It's infectious – the* OTHERS *join in.*

MOULE. Why is this matter so diverting?

BROOKS. Lawks, sir, last parson bisn't bothering with no water for no christening. He just spit in his old hand, and anoints the babe with that.

Pause.

MOULE. Mr Clerk. In Mark, chapter one verse nine, I think you'll find, the Baptist speaks of this sacrament, and says, 'I indeed have baptised you with water; but He shall baptize you with the Holy Ghost' . . . And in, again I stand to be corrected, John three five, the Saviour tells us that except a man be born of water and the spirit, he cannot enter in God's kingdom. I note from the evangelists two references to water, one to the Spirit, and one, synonymically, to the Holy Ghost. I see no reference to spit. The service will recommence in five minutes time, when there will be water in the font.

MOULE *is turning to go. A horrible wail from the* ORCHESTRA: *it is beginning to rehearse.*

What – is – that – noise?

BROOKS. Why, sir, 'tis the orchestra. 'Tis Wednesday, so she be practising.

MOULE. I – see.

He goes out.

JOHN LOCK. Well.

JANE WHITING. Well, then.

BROOKS. Well, I daresen wager what he'll think to she come Sunday.

1.2.2 **The Vicarage, Fordington.** *Enter* MRS MOULE, CAPT WILLIAM HENNING, 35, *and* MRS ANN HENNING, 26. MARY MOULE *is the same age as her husband. Their maid* ELLEN WRIGHT, *in her late 30s, is in attendance.*

ANN HENNING. So Mrs Moule, you really can't imagine what delights you have in store . . .

HENNING. The spring, of course, particularly . . .

MRS MOULE. Well, yes, the natural beauty of the countryside is, well, manifest . . . But I must admit it does concern us that the very *size*, the parish's extraordinary *circumference* . . . must make it hard for many to attend the church with any regularity, particularly in winter . . .

HENNING. Well, in fact, yes, there are times . . .

MRS MOULE. And, further, captain, we confess we find it strange, to say the least, that at his time of life the previous incumbent could have made even the most modest excursions through a large part of the benefice.

HENNING. Well, certainly . . .

ANN HENNING. I think, um, William, that Mrs Moule should know . . . that Mr Palmer, well, particularly in his latter years . . .

HENNING. Though of course a man much loved . . .

MOULE *has entered.*

MOULE. Well, yes, indeed, ma'am. I am growing daily more aware of the eccentricities of the latter years of Mr Palmer.

They look at him.

MRS MOULE. Henry, it is captain, and . . .

HENNING. Henning. I'm pleased to meet you, Mr –

MOULE. Enquiring as I have this very morning of a woman put up for a sponsor – a regular attender I was told, and indeed compared to many of her class and quarter more or less a paragon – enquiring as I did of her what were the gospels and being told that she was certain there were two: St Peter's and St Paul's.

Pause.

ANN HENNING. Well, yes, indeed, there is of course much ignorance, for which no doubt Mr Palmer bears his share of the responsibility. But, Mr Moule, I must assure you that if not his teachings then his works, his acts of kindness and of simple charity –

MOULE. Madam, I am a vicar in the Church of Christ, and thus confess we are accounted righteous before God not by our own deservings, but by the gift of faith, and that without that gift, our 'works' avail us nothing.

HENNING. Um . . .

MOULE. It is a privilege to meet you, Captain, Mrs Henning.

MOULE *goes quickly out. Pause.*

ANN HENNING. Um, Mrs Moule . . . I understand, your husband takes an interest in fossils. And – remains.

Pause.

MRS MOULE. Yes. Yes, he does.

ANN HENNING. Because –

HENNING. Because it is clearly fortunate that in that sense, if in no other, Mr Moule has found a suitable appointment, ma'am.

1.2.3 **St George's Church, Fordington,** *on Sunday, with a full* CONGREGATION, *which sings the last verse of 'Now thank we all our God'. They do not sing it well, but then, they are accompanied by the St George's Church Orchestra. During the verse, three very old* COMMUNICANTS *assemble at the altar rail, and* MR BROOKS *and* HENRY MOULE *converse.*

CONGREGATION.
> All praise and thanks for God
> The Father now be given
> The Son, and him who reigns
> With them in highest heaven,
> The one eternal God,
> Whom earth and heaven adore;
> For thus it was, is now,
> And shall be ever more.

Meanwhile:

MOULE. Tell me, Mr Clerk. Is the orchestra more than usually out of tune this morning?

BROOKS. Oh, no. I'd say that she be round middling, sir.

MOULE. I see. And may I ask, is it normal for there to be so few to take the sacrament on Communion Sunday?

BROOKS. Oh, I tell you sir, that's not too bad a number, for a morning, in the winter. Why, half the time, 'twixt Christmas Day and Candlemas, we be hard put to it to worret up any soul at all.

MOULE *looks at* BROOKS *before going to address the*
COMMUNICANTS. *The hymn comes to an end.* MOULE *goes to*
the FIRST COMMUNICANT.

MOULE. 'The body of our Lord Jesus Christ, which was given for
thee, preserve thy body and soul unto everlasting life. Take and
eat this in remembrance that Christ died for thee, and feed on
him in thy heart by faith with thanksgiving.'

He gives the wafer to the FIRST COMMUNICANT.

FIRST COMMUNICANT. Well, thank 'ee, parson.

MOULE *gives a slight look, but carries on, presenting the cup to the*
FIRST COMMUNICANT:

MOULE. 'The blood of our Lord Jesus Christ, which was shed for
thee, preserve thy body and soul unto everlasting life. Drink this
in remembrance that Christ's blood was shed for thee, and be
thankful.'

FIRST COMMUNICANT (*taking the wine*). Best o'health, Jesus.

MOULE (*to the* SECOND COMMUNICANT). 'The body of our – '
what did you say?

FIRST COMMUNICANT. I said, 'best o'health, Jesus', sir. Be
summat wrong?

MOULE. Is something wrong?

SECOND COMMUNICANT. Ees, sir. Bissen us drinking health
of Our Lord Jesus?

MOULE. Drinking *what*?

FIRST COMMUNICANT. Ar. S'right. Old parson he do say
hisself. Communion be drinking Jesus' health.

THIRD COMMUNICANT. Right. Your best o'health, Jesus.

SECOND COMMUNICANT. Cheers, lord.

MOULE *almost snatches the cup back from the* SECOND
COMMUNICANT *and puts it on the table. He turns to* BROOKS,
in fury:

MOULE. Well, Mr Brooks?

BROOKS. Well, yes, indeed. Quite regular. Would you be wanting 'Glory be on high' now, Mr Moule?

As the ORCHESTRA *begins to play,* MOULE *climbs quickly into the pulpit.*

1.2.4. **St George's, Fordington.** MOULE *addresses the* CONGREGATION.

MOULE (*silencing the* ORCHESTRA). Thank *you.* May the words of my mouth, and the meditations of all our hearts, be now and forever acceptable in thy sight, O Lord, our strength and our Redeemer. Now.

He surveys the CONGREGATION.

Now, before I proceed to the main body of my sermon, I have a statement to make concerned with the proceedings of this church, and some changes which are in my opinion long overdue.

First of all, from now on, the font will be employed solely for the purpose of baptism – for which purpose water will be provided – and not as a receptacle for the headgear of the male members of the congregation.

Second. From this day forth, in addition to the morning Sunday service, there will be evening prayer on Sundays and on Wednesdays, and communion will be heard monthly. Further, communicants will not be paid sixpence or indeed any sum at all for taking the sacrament, and will do so in a manner and with words appropriate to its solemnity.

He clears his throat.

And finally . . . From today, I have decided that the orchestra will be suspended, and replaced by a, a seraphine, to be purchased by myself and played by Mrs Moule. My text today is taken from One Timothy: 'Let the elders that rule well be counted worthy of double honour, especially those who labour in the word and doctrine. Let as many servants as are under the yoke count their own masters worthy of all honour, that the name of God and doctrine be not blasphemed.'

A MUMMER *is seen.*

DRAGON. I say that you speak very bold
　　　　To such a man as I.
　　　　I'll cut you into eyelet holes
　　　　And make the buttons fly!

1.2.5. **The Vicarage.** MRS MOULE *admits a delegation from the* ORCHESTRA. *The men carry instruments in green cases. They are* WILLIAM BARTLETT, *an old man,* WILLIAM FUDGE, *in his mid-40s, and his son* EDWARD, *17.*

BARTLETT. Ah, Mrs Moule.

MRS MOULE. Why, Mr –

BARTLETT. Bartlett. And Mr William Fudge. And his young Edward. And we be wondering if we might see the parson.

MRS MOULE. Yes, I'm sure.

　　MOULE *appears.*

MOULE. Ah, gentlemen. Forgive me, I was in the garden. Now, what can I do for you?

BARTLETT. Mr Moule, we've been a-considering of your announcement of last morning.

MOULE. Yes?

BARTLETT. And we hope that we might strike a bargain, like.

MOULE. A bargain?

BARTLETT. Mr William Fudge.

WILLIAM FUDGE. Mr Moule. Us do know that playing is uncommon rough, particular in wind, and 'tis true tidden fitting. Fact, we been a-trying to unwriggle old Bill Swyer from his serpent now for many a year.

BARTLETT. And fluster Joseph Normal off his flute.

WILLIAM FUDGE. That's right. So sir, our offer's this. We'll stop up her wind, and just be the strings.

　　Pause.

MOULE. Uh, well. I'm of course delighted that you have been considering matters with – consideration. But I'm afraid that I remain of the opinion that from now on the singing should be accompanied by seraphine.

Pause.

BARTLETT. Ar. Excuse us for one moment, if you would.

MOULE. Of course.

The MEN *go into a huddle, a little apart.* MOULE *looks at* MRS MOULE. MRS MOULE *gives a slight smile.* BARTLETT *turns back to* MOULE.

BARTLETT. Now, Mr Moule. We've a-been given theasan matters some further considering, and us have resolved –

WILLIAM FUDGE. Reluctantly –

BARTLETT. Ees, with reluctancy, to make a further proposal, like.

MOULE. Yes, what is it?

BARTLETT. Mr Fudge.

WILLIAM FUDGE. Our offer is, we do break up the orchestra, but us stay up in the gallery, leading the singing, as us always has.

Pause.

MOULE. Yes. But I'm afraid, still, I do feel that the whole congregation should be – and sing – in the body of the church. Together.

BARTLETT. Hm. Forgive us for one further moment, if you would.

MOULE. Indeed.

The same: the huddle of conference, and a smile from MRS MOULE. BARTLETT *leads his* MEN *back.*

BARTLETT. Now, sir. We do have to tell you, that we be unanimously resolved, that if the concluding of this business were to be as you might say *postponed* like –

MOULE. Look, I'm sorry, but I have considered this most

carefully myself. I had hoped that what I heard at first was just an aberration. But it is clear, however, that the standards I have witnessed are the standards which obtain, and I must insist that the changes I have announced are implemented.

Pause.

BARTLETT. I do see.

MOULE. I'm glad.

WILLIAM FUDGE. These be your last words, then, like.

MOULE. Yes.

BARTLETT. Well, then. So be it.

WILLIAM FUDGE. You're certain –

MOULE. I'm absolutely certain.

BARTLETT. Well, we'll be a-wishing you a good day, then.

MOULE. Good day.

The delegation leaves. WILLIAM FUDGE *has left his violin case, but neither they nor the* MOULES *notice.* MRS MOULE *smiles.*

Well, there we are.

MRS MOULE. 'With *great* reluctance . . .'

MOULE. Yes, in fact, 'reluctancy . . .'

MOULE'*s amused too. Neither notice the re-entrance of* EDWARD FUDGE.

EDWARD FUDGE. My father left his fiddle.

He picks up the green case.

He didn't like to come for she hisself.

MOULE. Please, I –

EDWARD FUDGE. I think, sir, if you'll excuse me saying, you will regret what you do say here this afternoon.

Slight pause.

MOULE. Oh, I assure you, Edward –

EDWARD FUDGE. Like it might be as you'll come to see things from a different angle, in the course of time.

MOULE. Well, Edward, I must say, I find it hard –

EDWARD FUDGE. Like the angle of an old man on eight shillen for a full week in the fields. And with the threat like hanging over he, that with the threshers and the winnowers and such, he'll lose his hire and house and end up God knows where.

Slight pause.

Like what a fiddle on a Sunday means to he. Good afternoon, then, reverend.

He turns and goes.

Scene Three

1.3.1. **Dorchester High St,** *from the Vicarage of Fordington, up High St East and High St West, to the Barracks at the Top'o'Town. This scene represents* MOULE'*s walk from the Vicarage to the Barracks, during which he passes representatives of most of the social classes of the borough: by the end, they will form both a geographical and social 'map' of the town.*

NARRATIVE. And such was the abrasive manner of the Reverend Henry Moule,

that by the time that he accepted a commission to preach weekly at the Barracks

there was hardly anyone who saw him on his brisk walk through the town

who did not know him as a man of the most unaccommodating creed,

if not an actual Methodist.

MOULE *appears from the Vicarage, to meet* NATTY SEALE, *a shepherd of indeterminate age, wearing a moleskin cap, smock, and leggings.* NATTY *is accompanied by his sheep* CAROLINE.

NATTY. Good morrow to you, parson.

MOULE. Morning, Mr –

NATTY. Seale. Name's Natty Seale. Tell Natty by he's hat. Bissen none in old Ford'n as don't know I, and me old friend Caroline.

Pause.

Say I a buggalug or gallypot, they do say. But I bissen.

He waves the tail of his hat at the sheep.

Tell by he.

MOULE. Well, church is at eleven, Mr Seale. I'll doubtless see you there.

NARRATIVE. And then left on to High East St where

MOULE *passes* INNKEEPERS, *including* ANN BESANT, *50, and* CHARLES *and* SARAH ELDRIDGE.

the widow Ann Besant, proprietor of the White Hart coaching inn, is testing her best Sunday brew.

ANN BESANT. Good health to you then, parson!

NARRATIVE. A barrel rolls in from the backyard to the Phoenix taproom –

LANDLORD. Morning!

NARRATIVE. And catching sight of no less a couple than the Eldridges,

SARAH. beerhouse keepers,

CHARLES (*reminding his wife*). but with eyes on higher things,

NARRATIVE. as they made their way into All Saints' Church for early service.

Just a moment between MOULE *and* SARAH: *a nod, a bob and they pass on. Now we are half way up the High St, at the point where East gives way to West, and* MOULE *passes the* PROFESSIONAL CLASSES, *including* MR PATCH *the Music Teacher,* CAPT *and* MRS HENNING, *the middle-aged* HENRY FRAMPTON *and his aunt* MRS MARY FRAMPTON.

NARRATIVE. Towards which place of worship came not only the professional classes,

surgeons,

and solicitors,

PATCH. and music teachers and the like,

MRS FRAMPTON. but also Mrs Mary Frampton and her nephew Henry,

NARRATIVE. with their friends the Hennings;

who following their first and only call on Mr Moule,

ANN HENNING. had determined to transfer their spiritual custom

HENNING. to more congenial surroundings.

In the 'Barracks' itself, CAPT AUGUSTUS HANDLEY, *24, sits proudly on a* HORSE. *We do not immediately notice he is fast asleep.*

NARRATIVE. And thence to Top'o'Town, and to the Barracks,

where Mr Moule said Morning Prayer and preached a sermon;

and, his congregation having been dismissed,

he picked up the guinea from the drumhead,

and turned to go.

1.3.2. **The Barracks.** AUGUSTUS HANDLEY *gives out a horrible groan.*

MOULE. Um – Captain –

HANDLEY. Uh . . .

MOULE. Can I help you, Captain?

CAPT HANDLEY *slides gently off the* HORSE *onto the floor. The* HORSE *neighs.* HANDLEY *looks up.*

HANDLEY. Ah. Padre. Morning.

He tries to stand. An error.

In the name of *Christ* –

He looks at MOULE.

I'm sorry.

MOULE. Oh, Captain, don't apologise to me. I cannot save your soul from everlasting fire, unless you honestly repent you of your blasphemy.

HANDLEY. Beg pardon?

MOULE. I know. It must seem hard. All you did was take the Lord's name in vain, and even then, not in a particularly outrageous fashion. But, in fact, sin has nothing to do with harm, or injury to other men. It is offending against God, by flouting His great law, and thus the lightest of profanities is on a level with the worst of murders. Quite literally, sin is sin, its wages death.

MOULE *smiles pleasantly*. HANDLEY *climbs to his feet*.

HANDLEY (*a little irritated*). Well, if it's of any comfort, padre, at this moment I feel very close to death, and –

MOULE. Oh, no comfort, Captain. For even if you at this very moment spurned all sin, it would be nothing worth, unless through faith and faith alone you do accept God's grace, without which, as Isaiah preaches, 'all our righteousness is but as filthy rags'.

Pause. HANDLEY *tries to go for lightness*.

HANDLEY. Well, certainly –

MOULE *has taken a penknife from his pocket, and thrusts it at* HANDLEY.

MOULE. Captain. This is my penknife. Take it.

HANDLEY. I'm sorry?

MOULE. I offer you my penknife. Do you accept it?

HANDLEY. No, of course I don't.

HANDLEY *looks at the vicar holding out a penknife to him*.

I mean . . . What do you mean?

MOULE. I mean . . . That from birth you are a child of wrath, from birth you run astray, choosing the company of strangers. And unless you are offered, and *accept* His grace, as I offer you this penknife, then you will remain, cursed, in that company for all eternity.

Pause.

HANDLEY. I mean . . . I can't.

Pause.

I mean . . . Forgive me, padre.

Scene Four

1.4.1. **Outside St George's, Fordington.** MOULE *joins* MRS MOULE, *their servant* ELLEN WRIGHT, *and their two small boys,* HENRY JNR, *nine, and* GEORGE, *six. Round the church gate wait a number of* ROUGHS, *including* LIZZIE *and* JANE SIBLEY *(15 and 20). Aside, watching, are* FLORENCE CHAFFLEY, *11,* JANE WHITING, NATTY SEALE *and* MARTHA LOCK.

NARRATIVE. And so Henry Moule returned to East Fordington, to collect his wife and family for Morning Prayer:

and to find himself confronted by another delegation.

MOULE *leading his* FAMILY *into church, through a gauntlet of the* YOUNG ROUGHS.

YOUNG ROUGHS (*variously*).
    Eh. Here they comes.
    Who?
    Parson. Parson's missus.
    Ooh. Look at t'black face on'n.
    Eh. And parson's lambs.
    Baa baa.
    Baa baa!

SOMEONE *grabs at* GEORGE's *cap.*

YOUNG ROUGH. Eh look 'is pretty cap.

LIZZIE SIBLEY *grabs at* HENRY JNR's *cap.*

LIZZIE SIBLEY. And this un's too.

They play catch.

JANE SIBLEY. Eh, here to I!

JANE WHITING. Here's to your best health parson!

YOUNG ROUGHS. Baa baa! Baa baa! Parson's lambs! Baa baa!

The MOULES *are through. Bravely, though from a distance,*
ELLEN WRIGHT *turns back and shouts:*

ELLEN WRIGHT. You be the devil's sheep you be!

Catcalls and laughter, as the ROUGHS *sing:*

YOUNG ROUGHS. Hokey, pokey, winkey, wum,
      How d'ye like your teaties done?
      All to pieces, that's the fun –
      Can ye now just gie I one?

NARRATIVE. And even after Church, the protests were not over.

as the citizens of Fordington continued to display their dim
opinion of the Reverend Moule:

from the landowners and gentry who declined to call,

to those who made their views known more directly.

1.4.2. **The Vicarage.** *Night.* MRS MOULE *appears to* MOULE,
her arms full of dead flowers and vegetables, ripped up by the roots.

MOULE. Mary, what is it?

MRS MOULE. What do you think? They're flowers, from the
garden. And the vegetables. Ripped up and scattered.

Pause.

And they pulled the railings up. And they broke into your shed,
and smashed your specimens.

Pause.

MOULE. So, did you see them?

MRS MOULE. No. But I heard them. Heard them, clear as clear.
'Oh hokey pokey, winkey wum. How do you want your taters
done?'

MOULE *embraces* MRS MOULE.

MOULE. Oh, Mary, this will end.

MRS MOULE. I know. I know.

A cough. MARTHA LOCK *appears.*

MOULE. Who's there?

MARTHA LOCK. Uh – parson –

MOULE. I'm sorry? Mrs Lock?

MARTHA LOCK. Uh, parson. I just wanted – I did want to say
. . . As how it's not everyone as holds with they around the
church a-Sunday.

Slight pause.

And they do say it's being's they be so poor. But with that I
can't agree. For there's always summat left for spending in the
public house, or for betting at the races. And I may not be that
regular a churchgoer. But I do know sin is sin, its wages death.
And whatever be their circumstances, they will die and suffer
everlastingly. As it is written, Mr Moule.

MARTHA LOCK *hurries out.* MOULE *embraces his wife.*

MOULE. For everyone that asks receives. For everyone who seeks
shall find.

Scene Five

1.5.1. **The Green Dragon Parlour.** *It is 1833.* SARAH, *who is
carrying a baby, enters with a manuscript, followed by* CHARLES.
CHRISTIAN *their servant is filling jugs and mugs of beer, to take
them through to the public bar.* SARAH's *manuscript is the draft of an
advertisement.*

SARAH. Right. First of all: CHARLES ELDRIDGE. Big. In
capitals.

CHARLES. I see.

CHRISTIAN *is watching, open-mouthed, as* SARAH *reads the
advertisement: so much so that she allows a jug to overflow.*

SARAH. CHARLES ELDRIDGE has the honour to announce to
the nobility, the gentry, and all readers of the *Dorset County
Chronicle* oh do be *careful* Christian –

CHRISTIAN. Ooh. Ooh, sorry, ma'am.

She carries the tray off. A look shared between SARAH *and*
CHARLES. CHRISTIAN *will return for another load a little later.*

SARAH. – that he is upon the 7th of November 1833 to enter upon proprietorship of the Antelope Hotel in Cornhill, Dorchester, and hopes that by sparing neither pains nor expense – that should be '*trusts* that' . . . by sparing neither la-di-da to render it one of the first houses in the West of England.

CHARLES (*as if that's it*). Very good. When does it –

SARAH. Mercy, I've not begun.

CHARLES. You've not?

SARAH. By no means. Carry on.

She hands the manuscript to him and he carries on reading.

CHARLES. As a FAMILY HOTEL,

SARAH. – in capitals,

CHARLES. – the Antelope possesses very superior accommodation . . .

This is not a universally accepted truth. CHARLES *looks dubiously at* SARAH.

Well –

SARAH. Read on.

CHARLES (*with increasing incredulity*)   . . . having been utterly re-embellished and repaired and now possessing every requisite for comfort and convenience?

SARAH (*sweetly*). Five weeks.

CHARLES. The most complete accommodation is afforded to travellers by COACH from Bath and London and to Exeter and Weymouth . . . The STABLING is of a first-rate character, with experienced ostlers and the best of corn and hay –

SARAH *reads over his shoulder as* CHRISTIAN *carries a tray of mugs across – a nerve-wracking spectacle.*

SARAH. The DINING ROOMS will be supplied with the finest production of the respective seasons.

CHARLES. While the TABLES will be served by active and steady waiting staff.

They look at CHRISTIAN, *then each other.*

SARAH. Well, yes, we may well have to let her go. So that's it. Well, thus far.

CHARLES. Thus far?

SARAH. Like, that's the first.

CHARLES. First? Of how many?

SARAH. Five. One a week. For five weeks. So that nobody in Dorchester won't know that Charles Eldridge, formerly steward to Mr Robert Williams of Little Bredy, do be appointed by that same Mr Robert Williams to manage his famed Coaching Inn the Antelope, of Cornhill, Dorchester.

The Antelope, the setting of no less lustrous an occasion than the Annual Race Meeting Steward's Ordinary Dinner.

That's Mr Williams, of 'May I be the first to wish you every happiness'.

SARAH'*s eyes are blazing.* CHARLES *is caught up with her enthusiasm, and takes her in his arms.*

Oh, mercy, Charles. We've not begun.

1.5.2. **Mrs Mary Frampton's house.** MRS FRAMPTON *is in conversation with* HENRY MOULE.

MOULE. Madam, I speak what must be plain to you. These 'races' are a sport, or rather an amusement, which bring good to no one, but misery to many; which are a great promoter of both drunkenness and fornication, and whose very essence is gambling. How can it not be manifest, to a Christian woman –

MRS FRAMPTON. Mr Moule.

Pause.

Mr Moule. You have closed down your church orchestra, you have distressed one portion of your congregation, and you are an object of the rankest ridicule to the other, and now you wish me, in public association with your name, to withdraw my patronage from one of Dorchester's most popular festivities.

MOULE. Mrs Frampton, I must assure you, with the greatest

possible sincerity, that popular or no –

MRS FRAMPTON. Mr Moule, I must assure you I am in no
doubt of your sincerity. But I can go no further than to say that
I will observe this year's race meeting with the utmost diligence.
There's really nothing more to say.

Pause. MOULE *gives a slight bow.*

MOULE. Well, I – I thank you, ma'am.

He turns to go.

MRS FRAMPTON. Mr Moule, may I ask if you're aware of the
extent of your unpopularity, even among the gentler classes?

MOULE. I am aware, ma'am. I cannot wholly understand it.

MRS FRAMPTON. Well –

MOULE. I have always striven to uphold legitimate authority.
Indeed I believe that to be one of the sources of hostility towards
me and my family.

MRS FRAMPTON. Well, yes, of course. But, nonetheless, your
doctrine is a harsh and unforgiving one. It does not speak to men
and women as they are. And they'll not thank you for assuring
them that as they are, they're damned.

MOULE. Well, ma'am, I do not wish for thanks.

MRS FRAMPTON. Well, Mr Moule, I'm glad of that, for
otherwise I fear you will be often disappointed.

Scene Six

1.6.1. **Maiden Castle: Dorchester Races.** *The races are held on the
ancient earthwork just outside the town. It is September 1835.*

NARRATIVE. September 1835!

Maiden Castle!

Dorchester Races!

To the Music of the Regimental Band of the Seventh Lancers!

And suddenly, the RACES *are everywhere, and almost every
character we have met – with the exception of the* MOULE *family –*

could be here. Certainly, SPECTATORS *include* MRS
FRAMPTON, HENRY FRAMPTON *and the* HENNINGS;
CAPT AUGUSTUS HANDLEY; ANN BESANT, *who runs a
beertent;* CHARLES ELDRIDGE, *who patronises it; and, from
Fordington, at least* JANE *and* LIZZIE SIBLEY. *There is also
much else happening, at many stalls, and some or all of the following
could be going on, in addition to the* MUSICIANS, *from the*
REGIMENTAL BAND *to* HURDYGURDYMEN *and*
GYPSIES *playing on fiddles and spoons.*

FIRST BOOKIE. Come on then sonnies, come on then, what
d'you know, here's evens on this good thing, I'm giving evens on
Miss Careful and a bottle on Anticipation, sonnies, over here . . .

SECOND BOOKIE. Right I'm not giving evens I'm giving two to
one the jolly, Miss Careful the Jolly and I'm taking on six to four
the Sultan, eleven to one outside Bacchanal . . .

ANN BESANT. Best beer here! Best Besant beer for three farthen!
That's three farthen for a pint, and a ha'pence for a refill! Rum,
whisky and the finest wines! As retailed at the famous White
Hart Inn. Retailed right here exclusive!

MUMMIFIER. Form a line here, for the Egyptian mummy! After
three thousand years clasped in the clammy grasp of death, to be
revived and recalled to life for the very first time before your
very eyes! Separate showings at three o'clock precisely, half past
three, and each half hour thereafter! The price reduced by a full
quarter so to place this novel treat within the reach of all!

PIGMAN. Line up here, gentlemen and ladies, for the greatest
curiosity of this or any age, Toby, the world-famed Sapient Pig.
Who will in front of you and with no aid of any kind read, spell,
play cards, and cast accounts; tell any person what o'clock it is,
and to the minute, and the age of any one in company!

TEST STRENGTH. So, gennlemen. So lads. Who'll test his
strength against the notorious Tattooed Man of Tomboctoutu! A
pound of baccy to the man holds out the longest, and a yellow
capon to the boy! Roll up here, for the famous man of
Tomboctoutu and his famous tattooed arm.

TATTOOED MAN. Not just me arm, mum, neither.

WAXWORKS. Ladies and gents! At vast expense, for your
enlightenment, we present Signora Capelli's famed Waxwork
Exhibition – containing as it does two Grecian Venuses – both
utterly dissectable in all their parts – and a parade of British
monarchs from the Conqueror unto the present day!

SECOND BOOKIE. . . . did I say six to four I now say two to
one on Sultan, that's a bottle on the Sultan, evens for the Jolly, a
shillen on the Sultan gets you two, and sixpence on the
Bacchanal you're swimming . . .

FIRST BOOKIE. . . . what d'you know he's down on Sultan, I'm
still showing you a bottle on Anticipation, a shillen'll get you
two, come on then sonnies, show your silver evens on the jolly,
get this good thing here . . .

NARRATIVE. And to the main event!

The high spot of the afternoon!

The Dorset Yeoman Stakes!

Ten sovereign each, with 25 added from the fund!

A handsome silver cup donated by the Steward!

And they're OFF!

And the ENTIRE ASSEMBLY *watches the race run around them,
shrieking for their* HORSES, *until the race is won, betting slips fly in
the air, the* ASSEMBLY *disperses, and only a carpet of paper is left.*

1.6.2. **A Corner of the Racecourse.** *On the nearly deserted
earthwork, the 12-year-old* FLORENCE CHAFFLEY *is selling bits
and pieces from a tray. A little apart,* MRS FRAMPTON *meets*
MOULE.

MRS FRAMPTON. Well, Mr Moule. I have fulfilled my promise.
But I must tell you honestly that I have seen nothing that can be
readily complained of.

CHARLES ELDRIDGE, *who has had a vinous afternoon,
approaches little* FLORENCE.

CHARLES. So, missie. What's this here?

FLORENCE. It's firewood, sir. And posies. Lemon balm.

CHARLES. Let's see your posies.

FLORENCE (*showing* CHARLES). They're a farden, sir.

CHARLES. Then I'll take three. And here's a penny for you.

FLORENCE. Thank 'ee, sir.

As he goes, CHARLES *overhears* MRS FRAMPTON *and looks quizzically towards* MOULE.

MRS FRAMPTON. And I therefore must inform you, in all conscience, and here upon this ancient site, I really cannot undertake to bring about the downfall of this harmless and traditional festivity.

Pause.

MOULE. You must do as your conscience guides you, Mrs Frampton.

He turns and goes. MRS FRAMPTON *turns to go in the opposite direction. Two* DRAGOONS *appear. One is* CAPT AUGUSTUS HANDLEY. *The other is a* SERGEANT. HANDLEY *is very much worse for wear. He stops.*

HANDLEY. Um – Sergeant.

SERGEANT. Sir.

HANDLEY. I am – I am waited for in Dorchester. For dinner.

SERGEANT. Is that so, sir.

HANDLEY. Yes.

The SERGEANT *looks quizzically at* HANDLEY, *who has shut his eyes.*

SERGEANT (*to himself*). Well, then. Bon appétit.

He walks on, leaving HANDLEY. *He comes to* FLORENCE. MRS FRAMPTON *still watches.*

FLORENCE. Uh – firewood, Captain? Mushrooms? Lemon balm?

SERGEANT. Well, maidy. And is that kindling that you're selling there?

FLORENCE. That's right, sir. It's three fardens, sir.

SERGEANT. And is kindling all you got on sale today?

FLORENCE. Sorry?

SERGEANT. 'Cos there's sixpence in it for you if it ain't.

Pause.

So what's your name.

FLORENCE. Be Florence. Florence Chaffley, sir.
There's a place back of the waxworks we can go.

FLORENCE *goes off quickly with the* SERGEANT. MRS
FRAMPTON, *horrified, hurries to* HANDLEY.

MRS FRAMPTON. Captain!

HANDLEY. Um – yes?

MRS FRAMPTON. Your sergeant, captain. And a girl. They went
that way. And you must *stop them.* Instantly.

HANDLEY. Uh – when you say, a girl –

MRS FRAMPTON. She can be no more than twelve, sir!

HANDLEY *grasps the situation and hurries in the direction* MRS
FRAMPTON *indicated. But he can see nothing. He turns back
towards* MRS FRAMPTON.

HANDLEY. Um – Uh, I'm so sorry, I . . .

MRS FRAMPTON. Captain, you should be ashamed.

Scene Seven

1.7.1. **The Antelope: Servery and Dining-Room.** *A sudden burst of
male noise from the dining-room establishes the Stewards' Ordinary
Dinner, at which the diners include* HENRY FRAMPTON, CAPT
HENNING, MR PATCH, *the elderly* ROBERT WILLIAMS, *the
young* LIEUT VANDALEUR, *and, by the time we move into the
dining-room,* CAPT HANDLEY. *At the moment, we are in the
servery, where* CHRISTIAN *is drawing corks from claret bottles. Other*
SERVANTS *bring through trays of dirty plates from the dining-room,
where the meal is just about completed.* SARAH, *who is pregnant,
enters the servery from the dining-room.*

SARAH. Now, Christian. Are the decanters in the market room?

CHRISTIAN. Yes, Mrs Eldridge.

SARAH. And the claret corks be drawn?

CHRISTIAN. Yes, ma'am.

SARAH. And do you see your master?

CHRISTIAN. Mr Eldridge? No, ma'am.

She picks up a tray of claret bottles.

Sorry.

SARAH (*briskly, taking the tray*). Well. No doubt before the evening is quite over –

CHARLES enters. CHRISTIAN sees him.

CHRISTIAN. Uh – uh, ma'am –

SARAH turns to see her husband.

SARAH. Why, Charles.

Slight pause. CHRISTIAN skuttles out.

Charles, it be near to half past seven.

CHARLES. Ah. Is dinner served?

SARAH. And eaten. Charles, are you –

CHARLES. I'm sorry.

He takes the posies from behind his back and presents them to SARAH.

Was I missed?

SARAH. Well, if I be absolutely honest with you, Charles, I'd have to say that things have got on cheerfully enough without you. If the truth be told.

A moment before ROBERT WILLIAMS enters from the dining-room.

ROBERT WILLIAMS. Well, good evening, Charles.

CHARLES takes the tray from SARAH, and proceeds past ROBERT WILLIAMS to the dining-room.

CHARLES. Good evening to you, Mr Williams.

SARAH (*half-whispered*). Charles . . .

But now ROBERT WILLIAMS *has reached her.*

ROBERT WILLIAMS. Mrs Eldridge. You must know, that your table has surpassed all expectation.

SARAH. Well, Mr Williams, naturally, 'tis not for me to judge.

ROBERT WILLIAMS. Well, no. But nonetheless, we *are* judged, as you know, throughout the town if not the county, as a most extraordinary success.

SARAH. Well, certainly, if we've achieved . . .

ROBERT WILLIAMS. From every quarter, I receive most glowing compliments. I nod, I smile. I bask, in your reflected glory.

CHRISTIAN *re-enters from the market room.*

SARAH. . . . then it must be down to you. Your generosity, and faith in us.

ROBERT WILLIAMS. Indeed. My confidence that what is past is past. A confidence most amply justified.

SARAH *is unsure of what* WILLIAMS *is implying. In the dining-room, there is a chant of 'cloth, cloth'.*

SARAH. Well, certainly –

ROBERT WILLIAMS. But hark. The cloth is called for. You'll forgive me, Mrs Eldridge.

He smiles and goes back in to the dining-room. SARAH *looks perplexed.*

CHRISTIAN. So who's that, ma'am?

SARAH. That, Christian, be Mr Robert Williams. The owner of this here hotel.

CHRISTIAN. What, Mr Robert Williams of *Little Bredy*?

SARAH (*beginning to move*). Yes. That's it.

She goes into the dining-room as HENRY FRAMPTON *finally demands the cloth.*

FRAMPTON. Gentlemen. Gentlemen. The cloth.

There are cheers, and then an accelerating chant, as CHARLES *prepares to, and then does, whisk the cloth off the table, with an alarming flourish.*

THE GENTLEMEN. Cloth, cloth, cloth, cloth, cloth!

Applause. FRAMPTON *strikes his gavel for silence. He proposes the first toast.*

FRAMPTON. Gentlemen. His Majesty.

ALL. His Majesty.

HENNING. The continued glory of his Forces here and overseas.

ALL. Continued glory. Forces.

VANDALEUR. *Particularly* the Seventh Lancers.

ALL. *Particu*lancers.

PATCH. The prosperity of Dorchester, its professional, commercial and agricultural endeavours!

ALL. Prosperry Dorch and agrideavours!

FRAMPTON. And naturally – the races!

ALL. The races!

FRAMPTON. Now, Mr Patch?

ALL. Yes, Patch! Song! Mr Patch!

PATCH *stands with studied diffidence.*

PATCH. Um – Spotted Cow? Sheepcrook and Black Dog?

SOME (*variously*). Spotted Cow!
No, the Hawk! Grey Hawk!

The Grey Hawk has it. MR PATCH *clears his throat and begins. During the song.* CHARLES *and* SERVANTS *pour wine for the* GENTLEMEN.

PATCH. Once I had a grey hawk,
        And a pretty grey hawk,
        A sweet little bird of my own,
        But she took a flight,
        She flew away quite,

> And nobody knows where she's gone,
>> my brave boys,
> There's nobody knows where she's gone.

Once the song is established, WILLIAMS *whispers to*
FRAMPTON, *who smiles and goes with him to* SARAH
ELDRIDGE.

ROBERT WILLIAMS. Now, Mrs Eldridge. Let me introduce you
to the Steward.

SARAH. Captain Frampton. It's the greatest honour.

FRAMPTON. Well, Mrs Eldridge, I must own, that after this –
extraordinary display, the 'honour' is all mine –

ROBERT WILLIAMS *is returning to his seat, as there is a banging
at the table, and the song begins to grind to a halt.*

Not that, I fear, that everyone is in a fit condition to appreciate –

*Both he and the song are brought to a halt by the insistent banging of
a mug on the table. To everyone's considerable surprise – if not horror
– it appears that* CHARLES ELDRIDGE *has abandoned his
hosterly duties, and has resolved to address the assembly.*

What's this?

CHARLES. Gentlemen, gentlemen.

Silence.

Gennlemen.

VANDALEUR. Who's this?

HENNING. It's Eldridge. Landlord.

VANDALEUR. Should he, um –

CHARLES. Far be it from your humble host to interrupt an
occasion of such – manifest convil – conviviality . . .

SARAH. Oh no.

CHARLES. But I view it as imperative, that everyone is made
aware of the danger in which we are all – situated.

PEOPLE *look round, nervously.*

For even within half a mile, at the Parish Church of Fordington,

St George, I say there lurks, a viper – snake in the grass – who has set himself the task and purpose to destroy, to cancel, to emil – eliminate, these races. These, our races.

Pause.

And this Ordinary.

Pause.

And with this fell purpose. And with this in mind. Has canvassed.

He's swaying. ROBERT WILLIAMS *stands.*

ROBERT WILLIAMS. Charles. For God's sake, sit down.

CHARLES. Or is that – can*vassed*?

He looks around. He realises where he is. He picks up the wine bottle and jug with which he's been serving the COMPANY, *and tries to carry on where he left off. He slumps, virtually on* VANDALEUR. *It's obvious he's gone.*

VANDALEUR. Give us a hand here, Captain.

HANDLEY. Yes, of course.

HANDLEY *comes and helps. They get* CHARLES *up and out.*

VANDALEUR. Now, all right, Mr Eldridge. Steady as she goes.

They've gone. SARAH, *superhumanly:*

SARAH. Now, gentlemen. May I suggest, there are spirits laid out in the market room . . .

The COMPANY *disperses to the other room.*

HENNING. Quite unbelievable.

PATCH. Well, certainly – most singular.

HENNING. Indeed.

FRAMPTON *and* ROBERT WILLIAMS *remain.*

FRAMPTON. Mrs Eldridge, I – I had been going to say . . . that I was sure that this would be the first of, first of many . . .

SARAH. Well, I'm not sure that's appropriate, now is it, Captain.

FRAMPTON. No. No, no.

He turns and goes. ROBERT WILLIAMS *comes to* SARAH.

ROBERT WILLIAMS. I'm very sorry.

SARAH. Yes. We will of course move out the instant you have found a replacement.

ROBERT WILLIAMS. Well, naturally, it would be in the interests of all parties . . .

SARAH. And then, I suppose, 'tis, back to the old Dragon.

She tries a little smile.

ROBERT WILLIAMS. He did – when he left my service, Mrs Eldridge – he did *swear* to me –

SARAH. What, that 'the past' was past? Well, yes.

Half to herself, with bitterness:

'Well, Mrs Balson. I do think I have the head for that.' Well yes, indeed.

HANDLEY *has reentered.*

HANDLEY. He'll be all right, now. He's asleep.

SARAH. Why, thank you, Captain.

ROBERT WILLIAMS *slips quietly out.*

HANDLEY. It does, if you'll forgive me saying, it does seem – a shame. It does just seem, to me, a terrible, great shame.

SARAH. Oh, 'tis just – what you might call a hazard of the occupation, Captain. Yes, that's all.

Slight pause. SARAH *smiles weakly at* HANDLEY. *A moment between them. Then,* HANDLEY *makes to go into the market room, then changes his mind and goes out another way.* SARAH *sits, disconsolate. Enter* CHRISTIAN.

CHRISTIAN. Oh, I'm sorry, ma'am.

SARAH *turns to* CHRISTIAN.

SARAH. Well, it's happened. And I suppose we do have to make the best of it.

CHRISTIAN. But, ma'am. With your contrivances and plans.

Like, for the brewery, and all. It must be – well, a mortal let-down for you, ma'am.

SARAH. Oh, yes. 'Tis so.

SARAH *rubs her pregnant tummy.*

Well, one thing's for sure. If it's another girl, she's Sarah. After all, he's had his Charles.

CHRISTIAN. And a lovely one he is too, ma'am.

SARAH. Indeed.

Pause.

Oh, Christian. You know, they're going to build the railway line, to London. And to Bristol. And I think, you see, I think that in no time the world, the whole world will be moving like a rocket, at the most – tremendous speed. And it would – it just would a-been, so thrilling, to a-been a part of that. But still.

Pause. She makes to go.

CHRISTIAN. Ma'am, do you know what *I* do read, like in the paper?

SARAH. No?

CHRISTIAN. The comet, ma'am. The Halley comet. Like, I do reckon she do spin a sight faster even than the railway locomotive, wou'n you say?

SARAH *takes* CHRISTIAN *by the shoulders. As she speaks,* CHARLES *comes back in, unnoticed. He carries a glove puppet.*

SARAH. Let me tell you, Christian. We live, today, in the most thrilling times there's ever been. Because – we be that comet's children, Christian, you do hardly dare to snatch a peek at us, we fly so fast and beam so bright and dazzling in the sky.

And the only thing can stop us, Christian, is the weakness of our own imagination. Truthfully. Elsewise, there be no limit, to how far we can go.

She lets CHRISTIAN *go.* CHARLES *stands there watching.*

CHARLES. Well, you just wait. I'm right. You'll see.

SARAH *looks at* CHARLES.

About the vicar, trying to stop the races. You just wait.

SARAH *says nothing.* CHARLES *waves the puppet.*

CHARLES. I meant to show you. I do finish little Charles. All finished now.

Slight pause.

That comet. Sounds a sight too bright for me.

A moment. Then he goes.

SARAH (*to herself*). Oh, yes. As far as far.

SONG (*from off*). And there's nobody knows where she's gone,
my brave boys,
No, there's nobody knows where she's gone.

1.7.2. **The Vicarage.** *First of all, a light on* MRS MARY FRAMPTON, *speaking the text of a letter she has written to* MOULE. *Then fade up light on the Vicarage, where* MOULE *is watching* MRS MOULE *reading the letter.*

MRS FRAMPTON. 'Well, Mr Moule. It seems that you were right and I was wrong. After our brief meeting, I was witness to a spectacle which underlined in fullest measure your worst fears, and I have to tell you that I shall indeed withdraw my patronage from next year's meeting, and will encourage all my friends to do the same. Remaining, then, your most sincere supporter in this matter . . .'

MRS MOULE. 'Mary Frampton.'

MRS MOULE *folds the letter.* MRS FRAMPTON *disappears.*

MRS MOULE (*to* MOULE). What did she see?

MOULE. I've no idea.

A knock at the door.

What is the time?

MRS MOULE (*moving to the door*). It's very late.

MOULE. Is Ellen . . .

Enter ELLEN WRIGHT.

ELLEN WRIGHT. Ma'am, 'tis a – military cast of gentleman.

MRS MOULE (*with a glance at* MOULE). Well, show him in.

ELLEN *admits* AUGUSTUS HANDLEY.

HANDLEY. Mr Moule, I doubt if you remember. My name's
Augustus Handley.

MOULE. Why, yes, of course. Do, please . . .

HANDLEY. And I would like – I would consider it the greatest
privilege . . . if you still possessed a penknife, Mr Moule . . .

Scene Eight

1.8.1. **Dragon Inn and Brewery; Fordington Vicarage.** *An
antiphonal, narrative scene between the* ELDRIDGES *and the*
MOULES.

NARRATIVE. And in the years that followed Sarah Eldridge set
about to build what she resolved would be the biggest brewery in
Dorsetshire . . .

SARAH *has entered with papers to* CHARLES.

SARAH. Now, Charles, first of all, I want to buy a mash-tun of
decent size. Indeed, 'tis more important than a second copper,
because I can use the one for water and for wort. Now, there be
a coopering concern in Poole . . .

She sees his face.

I'm sorry. First of all, I suggest *we* buy a mash-tun of decent
size . . .

NARRATIVE. And having built new premises behind the Dragon
malthouse, was quickly in production of 30 barrels of best beer a
day.

SARAH *is in conversation with* ANN BESANT.

SARAH. Now, my dear Mrs Besant, the thing is, not that your
brew is not delicious, which 'tis . . . I do never countenance the
view it's always dark and cloudy, that's certainly not *my*
experience . . .

ANN BESANT. Well, I should think not, Mrs Eldridge.

SARAH. But rather that however light and clear and sharp it may be, on occasions, that I can readily provide you, without a moment's worry, with a guaranteed and regular supply of beers and ales at what I'm sure you will agree to be the most attractive prices.

ANN BESANT. Well, Mrs Eldridge, I would need convincing of –

SARAH. – thus leaving you the time both to maintain and who knows to improve your service to the coaching and soon enough of course the railway trade. The service for which your establishment is nationally renowned.

NARRATIVE. While in Fordington, the Reverend Moule addressed the pressing need for the construction of a church or mission in the western reaches of his parish.

MOULE *with* MRS MOULE.

MOULE. Friends, I must report that I have once again approached the Council of the Duchy of Cornwall, who are as you know the major landowner, but I have to say that they have as before informed us they can offer no assistance in these straitened times.

NARRATIVE. Until, in 1846, two events occurred:

First, and despite the parsimony of the Duchy, the consecration of Christ's Church, West Fordington, under the charge of the recently-ordained Augustus Handley . . .

And second, the death of one Charles Eldridge, suddenly, of apoplexy, at the age of 55.

And now the two FAMILIES *have formed themselves into formal groups, like ceremonial photographs. On one side, in Fordington, are* MOULE, MRS MOULE *and* REV AUGUSTUS HANDLEY; *their teenage sons* GEORGE, HORACE *and* CHARLES; *and on the other, in Dorchester, the widowed* SARAH ELDRIDGE *and her children* SOPHIE, EMILY, CHARLES JNR *and* SARAH ALBINIA. *At the time of their father's death, they were 20, 15, 13 and 11 respectively, but for most of the subsequent action they are between four and eight years older. The two groups join in Psalm 90:*

PSALM. Lord, thou hast been our refuge: from one generation to another. Before the mountains were brought forth, or ever the earth and the world were made: thou art God from everlasting, and world without end. Thou turnest man to destruction: again thou sayest, come again, ye children of men.

During which:

NARRATIVE. And Henry Moule, now in his 46th year,

faced the continuing burdens of his ministry in the knowledge that those burdens were now shared . . .

While Sarah Eldridge, approaching 49,

confronted for the second time a life of widowhood,

and the knowledge that responsibility to keep her family

now rested in her hands alone.

The scene disperses, as:

While Dorchester itself prepared to welcome the arrival

marked by the most extensive public decoration,

and accompanied by regimental music and a seven-gun salute,

Of a most distinguished Royal Personage,

Borne for the first time in the county on the wings of locomotion, by the awesome and majestic power of steam . . .

And through the rising steam we see the first railway locomotive, bedecked with flags and accompanied by wild cheers from all sides, arrive in Dorchester.

Scene Nine

1.9.1. **The Dragon Brewery.** *It is 1850: the brewery is decked out for a celebration.* CHARLES JNR *stands in the middle, looking proudly around him.* CHRISTIAN *also stands there, beaming.*

CHRISTIAN. Well, Master Charles. Who would have thought it, eh? So fast. So *far.*

CHARLES *smiles at* CHRISTIAN. *Enter* EMILY.

EMILY. Now, Christian. Surely, you have twenty things to do.

CHRISTIAN. Yes. Yes, I'm sorry, Miss Emily.

She goes out, but doesn't miss a grin from CHARLES. EMILY
looks at her brother.

EMILY. If we're to be even half-way ready, Charles.

CHARLES *looks suitably abashed and goes out one way*, EMILY
another, as SARAH *and* SOPHIE *appear, putting up bunting.*

SARAH. John James? Ann's nephew? What? John James *Besant*?

SOPHIE. Mama, there's no need to affect such huge surprise. We
have been walking out for quite a time.

SARAH. And you do insist that your engagement is announced
tonight?

SOPHIE. Well, I never say '*insist*' –

SARAH. 'Neighbours and friends. I have brought you here to
celebrate a great new venture at the Dragon Brewery, the
harnessing of the great power of steam to the ancient art of beer-
making, oh and by the by my step-daughter Sophia's lost her
mind.'

SOPHIE. Oh, really now, mama!

CHRISTIAN *enters with a tray of pastries.*

SARAH. Ah, Christian.

CHRISTIAN. Ma'am?

SARAH. I don't see no bumpers. Could you bring some up?

CHRISTIAN. Yes, ma'am.

SARAH. Oh, and send Fanny to me, please.

CHRISTIAN. Yes, directly, ma'am.

SARAH. And – are those the pastries?

CHRISTIAN. Yes, ma'am.

SARAH *takes a pastry and eats it.*

Miss Emily was of the 'pinion I should lay 'en out in the
counting-room.

SARAH. Miss Emily was right.

CHRISTIAN *hurries on.*

Well, I suppose that if you are to marry this – this person, then tonight's as fine a time as any for me to seek the sympathy and comfort of my friends.

SOPHIE. Mama. What is amiss with John James? I mean, truly?

SARAH. Oh, nothing, nothing. Splendid fellow. The only brewer west of Salisbury who spends his leisure hours translating Ovid.

SOPHIE. Tacitus. Mama –

SARAH. Whereas, you know, your sister Emily –

SOPHIE. My sister Emily.

SARAH. – has been speaking most appreciatively of that young attorney whom we met in Melcombe Regis. Tizard, an old business family.

SOPHIE. Coal merchant.

SARAH. And the boy not 25, and already set upon a legal and political career.

FANNY LOCK *is the* ELDRIDGES' *second maid. She's in her mid-teens. She hurries in.*

Ah, Fanny.

FANNY. Yes, mm.

SARAH (*inspecting*). Now, do you have a clean bib for when the guests arrive?

FANNY. Of course, mm.

SARAH. Good girl. Now, do you please find Master Charles, and tell him that I want him to start up the engine now. Just to see that everything's in order. Right?

FANNY. Yes, mm.

FANNY *goes out.*

SARAH. While you on the other hand wish to attach yourself to this, to a sterling-silver gawk who's more or less in's dotage –

SOPHIE. Thirty two!

SARAH. – who appears to enjoy a much more intimate acquaintance with Thucydides and Cicero than with his relatives, his business or indeed the contemporary world.

Enter CHRISTIAN *with the glasses.*

Ah, Christian. Tell Mr Mason Master Charles is firing up the engine.

CHRISTIAN *makes to go in one direction.*

Mr Mason's somewhere in the brewery.

CHRISTIAN *makes to go in another direction.*

After the glasses, mind.

CHRISTIAN. Yes, Mrs Eldridge.

CHRISTIAN *moves off in a third direction.*

SARAH. Now –

SOPHIE. Mama, it's only that you don't share his opinions.

SARAH. Opinions?

SOPHIE. His interest in association and reform.

SARAH. Oh, yes, indeed. Well, I'd hoped that you'd a-learnt one thing of me, but clearly not.

SOPHIE. What's that, mama?

SARAH. It is, that one should entertain the most acute suspicion of a person spends more time a-worreting about *reform*, a-wallowing in all the pressing troubles of *society*, than bothering about the folks he actually knows, and things he might do summat practical about. Don't trust utopians. That's always been my policy.

SOPHIE. Mama!

SARAH. Because –

Screams from off.

Now, what?

Enter CHRISTIAN *in high alarm.*

CHRISTIAN. Oh, ma'am –

SARAH. Now, Christian, what –

CHRISTIAN. Oh, ma'am, it's Master Charles –

FANNY *runs through.*

SARAH. What's happened? Fanny?

CHRISTIAN. Oh, the blood!

SARAH. The *blood?*

Enter EMILY *and* SARAH ALBINIA.

EMILY. What's going on?

SARAH ALBINIA. Mama?

SARAH. Oh, Emily, your brother –

CHRISTIAN. Oh, Miss Sophie, you d'ave no idea . . .

SARAH. I must –

SARAH *is rushing towards the exit when* ALFRED MASON *hurries in. He's* SARAH's *brewer, 29 years old.*

CHRISTIAN. You cass'n picture it –

SARAH. Now, Alfred –

ALFRED. Sarah, it's all right. He's cut his foot, that's all.

SARAH. His foot?

CHRISTIAN. Great pools of it.

EMILY. Oh, Christian, do calm down.

CHRISTIAN. Like spurting . . .

SARAH. But, is somebody –

ALFRED. I've sent the new girl for the bandages.

SARAH. What, Fanny?

CHRISTIAN. And a-gushing, like you never see –

ALFRED. And he will be all right.

Enter FANNY *with water and bandages.* SARAH *turns to look at her. She doesn't understand the intensity of* SARAH's *look.*

FANNY. Uh – bandages.

SARAH. Right, thank you, Fanny. Thank you very much.

She grabs the bandages and hurries out followed by ALFRED, SARAH ALBINIA, SOPHIE *and* FANNY. CHRISTIAN *is still whimpering.*

EMILY. Oh, come on, Christian. Just a little blood.

EMILY *goes out.* GEORGE LODER *enters. He's in his late 40s. He's in his best clothes, and carries a letter. He looks around.*

CHRISTIAN. M'sorry, Miss Emily.

Ignoring LODER, CHRISTIAN *hurries out.*

GEORGE LODER. Um, 'scuse me . . . 'Scuse me . . .

He's alone. He looks round a little more. Enter SARAH.

SARAH. Christian! Christian, will you run for –

GEORGE LODER. Ah. Good evening. Mrs Eldridge?

SARAH. Yes, it is – Um, look, I'm sorry –

GEORGE LODER. Name be George Loder. I were sent this invitation.

SARAH. Yes, indeed. Now, Mr – Loder, you'll forgive me . . .

GEORGE LODER. From the Bull's Head.

SARAH. Bull's Head?

GEORGE LODER. Fordington.

SARAH. From *Fordington*. You're from the Bull's Head, *Fordington*.

GEORGE LODER. That's right.

SARAH. Well, Mr Loder. I'm delighted you could come. And first of all, I want to see you with a pint of Eldridge's best bitter in your hand. And then, I have a matter to discuss with you.

SOPHIE *has entered.*

SOPHIE. I think the bleeding's stopped, mama.

SARAH. Well, well. That's very good.

Pause.

That's excellent.

A moment. SOPHIE *moves in and takes her mother's hands.*

SOPHIE. I am not your daughter. You never knew my mother. Nor did I.

Slight pause.

But I still take heed of what you say. And I want to do what you think best.

Slight pause.

And I know that John James, tends to irk you, 'cos he hasn't really got a head for commerce, like . . . But, still, I love him. Like you loved my father, too.

Pause.

SARAH. Sophie. Your father was a kind man. But a weak one. And he thought that everybody was the same as him. And that's not just bad for business. Why, in these times, be downright dangerous.

SOPHIE *looks hard at her mother.*

You see, I thought I couldn't have a baby. So I married him for you.

She becomes aware that GEORGE LODER *is still there. To him:*

Forgive me, Mr Loder. We've been having something of a family crisis. And now I must go and see a silly boy.

She is moving quickly towards the exit when she confronts a MUMMER.

FIRST MUMMER. Is there a doctor to be found
　　　　　　　All ready, near at hand,
　　　　　　　To cure this dread and deadly wound,
　　　　　　　And make the champion stand?

SARAH *turns back, her face full of fear. She sees another* MUMMER.

SECOND MUMMER. Oh, doctor, doctor, play thy part:
　　　　　　　My son be wounded to the heart.

SARAH *quickly runs out, as a* THIRD MUMMER *appears.*

THIRD MUMMER. Oh George Prince George what have you
done?
You have slain your own beloved son.
You have cut him down like the evening
sun.

1.9.2. **Still the Brewery.** *The bunting still up, but some detached,*
hanging. SARAH *stands. Around her are* SOPHIE, EMILY,
SARAH ALBINIA, ALFRED MASON, JOHN TIZARD, *24, and*
JOHN JAMES BESANT, *32.*

SARAH. Who would have thought it. Just an itty-bitty little
scratch. And nothing for a week. And then his throat swell.
Mouth clamp shut. He arch up like a bow.

ALFRED. It's lockjaw, Sarah. Sometimes the blood's infected.
Nothing can be done. And nobody to blame.

SARAH. Oh, isn't there?

SOPHIE. No. *No,* mama.

SARAH *looks up at* SOPHIE. *Then she looks to* EMILY *and*
JOHN, *then to* SOPHIE *and* JOHN JAMES.

SARAH. I want you to get married. Both of you. I want my
grandchildren.

Pause.

Well, at least no change of wardrobe. I'm in black for Charles
already.

She looks at her daughters.

Like, having blinded both of them.

She goes out.

1.9.3. **Dorchester High St.** *The* CITIZENS *of the town, with*
handbills, read of an important forthcoming attraction.

CITIZENS. Oyez oyez.

Be it hereby known to all the patriotic citizens of Dorchester –

– and if there be any citizens of Dorchester who are not of the most patriotic cast of mind particularly at this hour of national peril we are yet to hear of them –

– that that most famous troupe, the Macarte Leviathan Equestrian Extravanganza –

– will represent in Salisbury Fields on Thursday next at five o'clock precisely –

– the heroic actions of our Turkish allies at the battle of the Danube basin and Silistra –

– following a Grand Procession through the town!

Scene Ten

1.10.1. **The Dragon Brewery: Parlour.** *August 1854. Enter* SARAH, EMILY, SOPHIE *and* SARAH ALBINIA.

SARAH. The Crimea. Don't talk to me about the Crimea.

EMILY. Mother. No one is talking to you about the Crimea. We're just reminding you that on Thursday John comes up from Weymouth for the Agricultural Society Dinner, and that Sophia and I could take Sarah Albinia to the equestrian parade.

SARAH. Shall I tell you what this war means to your mother? Ruin.

SOPHIE. Oh, mama. What do you mean?

SARAH. Well, first, of course, they march the soldiers off, and then they do pack the barracks with the only class of person in society denied my services –

EMILY *looks questioningly at* SARAH ALBINIA.

SARAH ALBINIA. They're convicts, from some London prison.

EMILY. Convicts?

SARAH. Yes. Yes, Fanny?

For FANNY LOCK *has entered.*

FANNY. Ma'am. It's the parson here to see you.

SARAH. Parson?

FANNY. Reverend Moule. From Fordington.

SARAH. Well, show him in . . .

>FANNY *goes out.*

>I'll see you three later.

>EMILY, SOPHIE *and* SARAH ALBINIA *go out as* FANNY *admits* MOULE.

>Why, Mr Moule.

MOULE. Well, Mrs Eldridge.

SARAH. You'll know our Fanny, doubtless: Fanny Lock. Her family lives down Mill Street.

MOULE. Oh, yes, I think I –

SARAH. And I'm sure she pays the closest possible attention to everything you tell her from the pulpit, don't you, Fanny?

FANNY. Yes, o'course, ma'am.

SARAH. Off you go.

>FANNY *goes out.*

>As good as gold. But still a trifle shy and awkward. Now, Mr Moule, I'm at full stretch for the harvest-home, so you'll please forgive me if we get straight down to business.

MOULE. Madam, it is of your servant's birthplace I would speak to you. Of Mill Street. Back of Ansty. Cuckold's Row. You know the area?

SARAH. Well, by repute.

MOULE. It is an area of considerable degradation.

SARAH. So I am told.

MOULE. Its population comes in large part from the countryside, and is now crammed into that tiny freehold of my parish which is not part of the demesne of the Duke of Cornwall.

SARAH. Well, I am not Prince Albert, Mr Moule.

MOULE. In many of the homes there is no possibility of even the most basic privacy. Most of the households draw their water from the millstream, an open channel of the vilest effluent.

SARAH. Nor, I regret, a sanitary inspector.

MOULE. The quarter is I tell you a repository of all that is unwholesome and immoral.

SARAH. Nor do I sit upon the Board of Guardians.

MOULE. No, madam, but you are a publican.

Pause.

SARAH. Indeed.

MOULE. Whose business is expanding. Dorchester, Cerne Abbas, Weymouth and beyond.

SARAH. I have purchased leases in those boroughs, yes.

MOULE. And in addition I am told the freehold of a public house in Fordington. 'The Bull'.

SARAH. The Bull's Head. Yes. The landlord, Mr Loder, is a person of the utmost probity.

MOULE. I wonder, then, how he squares his conscience with his trade?

Pause.

SARAH. Mr Moule. Let me be plain with you. I am a business person, one of modest means, who has just been through a harsh and unrewarding winter, and who now faces the evacuation of the military. I have to tell you that those setbacks leave me little room for charitable contributions. And indeed I must confess my view that as a man sows, may he reap, and that his conditions – even in the circumstances you describe – are his responsibility not mine.

MOULE. Oh, Mrs Eldridge, then we are at one. I do not see the salvation of the darker quarters of my parish in philanthropy.

SARAH. Well, I'm glad of that.

MOULE. Nor, I assure you, do I share the fashionable and dangerous opinion that men are immanently virtuous, and that their vice is merely consequent on circumstance.

SARAH. No more do I, I'm sure.

MOULE. I am convinced my parish cries out not for social but for moral restitution.

SARAH. Well, then we are agreed.

MOULE. And as drink is such an obvious contributor to the phenomena I have described, I must plead with you to cease your operations there.

Pause.

SARAH. Mr Moule, are you suggesting that I cease to trade in Fordington?

MOULE. In intoxicating liquors, yes.

SARAH. That's what I manufacture.

MOULE. And for the consequences of that fact are thus responsible.

SARAH. Might I suggest, therefore – that your quarrel might not be with me, but rather with those who consume my devil's brew –

MOULE. Oh, I have addressed them, madam. In yours and many other hostelries. There is a publication I retail on such occasions. Perhaps you'd accept a complimentary copy.

SARAH (*taking a tract from* MOULE). Thank you. D'you do a brisk trade, Mr Moule?

MOULE. No, I do not.

SARAH. In fact, I'd guess you comes in for a fair amount of ridicule. If not abuse.

MOULE. I have been victim to a certain – boisterousness, from time to time.

SARAH. Yes. Yes, I'm sure.

Pause. Then SARAH *has an idea. She goes and calls:*

SARAH. Sophie! Sarah Albinia! One of you, come here!

Enter SOPHIE.

SOPHIE. Yes, mama?

SARAH. Sophie, a glass of beer, please, for the vicar.

SOPHIE. Yes, at once.

She goes out.

MOULE. But, madam, I'm a –

SARAH. Yes. And if you choose not to accept my offer, I assure
you, I won't be offended in the least. You see, I sell rope, Mr
Moule. And people choose to buy it, or conversely not, and
spend their money in another way. And once they've got it, they
can use it to secure their property, or tow their vehicles, or for
all I know hold up their britches.

Enter SOPHIE *with a glass of beer.*

They can keep it coiled up in the attic, or they can swing upon it
from the rafters. But for the uses that they put it to, I am due
neither compliment nor blame. Why thank you, Sophie.

She takes the beer and drinks.

Your best health, Mr Moule.

MOULE. So I must conclude that I am misinformed.

SARAH. Oh, what about?

MOULE. About the cause of the untimely death of Mr Eldridge,
ma'am.

Pause.

SARAH. Mr Moule. My second husband – and my son – were
both called to their maker's arms before their time. They are
beyond the shadow of my judgement. And, if I may say so,
yours.

MOULE. But not beyond that of that very maker, ma'am. And as
I have repeated to those on the very rim of ruin, if a man
destroys himself by dissipation, vice or drunkenness, he is as
guilty as a suicide. And as Paul wrote to the Thessalonians, the
punishment for that is everlasting exile from the presence of the
Lord. There is, I must assure you, no reprieve.

Pause.

SARAH. Well, I'm sorry, but I can't believe that, Mr Moule.

MOULE. And I, too, am sorry, but it is really not a matter of

what you 'can' or 'can't' believe. In all solemnity, I must ask you
to consider the Epistle to the Hebrews, thirteen seven –

SARAH. No. No, thank you, Mr Moule –

SOPHIE. 'Remember them which have the rule over you, who
have spoken unto you the word of God . . . Jesus Christ, the
same yesterday, today and forever.'

MOULE. Yes.

SOPHIE. May *I* ask if you remember the first verses of that
chapter?

MOULE. I –

SARAH. No *more*.

Pause.

Now, really. I do really think, that it is now appropriate, for you
to go.

Pause. MOULE *gives a slight bow, turns to go, but then turns back.
Urgently*:

MOULE. It is – it is the babies, Mrs Eldridge. As a mother you
may understand. It is the babies, beaten by their fathers, or
abandoned by their mothers, found left on doorsteps, or – or
buried in back gardens, stuffed in ratholes by the river. There is
a woman in my parish, now thankfully reformed and in at least a
reasonably decent way of trade, who began to sell her body to
the soldiers in the taverns and the beertents, at the age of hardly
twelve. She'd lost three babies by the age of seventeen. And she
will bear no more.

Slight pause.

As you say, you sell rope, Mrs Eldridge.

He goes out. SOPHIE *goes to her mother.*

SOPHIE. Now, mama . . .

SARAH. Well. Really. What a – nonsense. How, absurd.

Slight pause.

Have we no Poor Laws? Boards for Public Health? I pay a
ransom to the Borough . . .

Slight pause.

No, I will not be blamed. I won't be held responsible.

SOPHIE. Mama –

SARAH. No, *don't*. Don't touch me. Don't.

She is fighting hard.

SOPHIE. Mama. D'you ever see one? Do you ever come across a
mother, down in Mill Street, with a baby she can't feed? With a
child who if it isn't fed will die?

SARAH. No. No, I haven't.

SOPHIE. Then – then isn't that utopian of *you*, mama.

Pause.

SARAH. Your mother died when she had you.

SOPHIE. I know. I was a stranger. And you took me in.

SARAH. No, no. You weren't a stranger. You were his. So you be
mine.

Pause.

That's right. There's nothing I can do. 'Cept waste time
wallowing in silly sentiment, 'bout folks I don't know and I can't
do nothing for.

She looks at SOPHIE.

I mean to say. The Reverend Moule, and Mill Street. Not our
parish. Not our business or concern. So what be they to us?

She looks to EMILY.

Where's Fanny?

SARAH *goes out.*

1.10.2. **Clifftops** *above the sea.* FANNY *and* HORACE *sit there,
looking down. They have a picnic.*

FANNY. Well, here we be. 'Tis the first time, this year, that I
don't go to the harvesting.

HORACE. Is that where you're supposed to –

FANNY. Right enough.

She looks out over the cliff.

HORACE. It's supposed to be a good one. Bounteous. This year.

FANNY. Well, cass'n be worse than last year, cans't it?

HORACE *smiles.*

HORACE. I don't know. I was in Oxford.

FANNY. Oxford. Well.

She looks out, over the sea.

The sea. 'Tisn't often I set eyes on her.

HORACE (*looking down*). That's Lulworth Cove. Our father used to take us there when we were children.

Slight pause.

FANNY. Well, I wonder what he'd think to you today?

HORACE. I daren't imagine.

FANNY. Saw him, yesterday.

HORACE. My father? Why?

FANNY. Came to see my mistress.

HORACE. At the brewery? Why, whatever for?

FANNY. Well, I dunno. I didn't overhear.

Slight pause.

But I don't doubt he've a way of getting what he's after. Reverend Moule.

Slight pause. HORACE *looks out to sea.*

HORACE. You know, from here, and on a day like this, you could imagine you could see, not France, or Spain, or Italy . . . But Athens, Constantinople. Or . . . Jerusalem.

He turns and smiles at FANNY.

You know?

Pause. FANNY *smiles back.*

FANNY. Like father, like son, eh?

Scene Eleven

1.11.1. **High St, Dorchester.** *And now the great* PROCESSION
enters, headed by the showman MR MACARTE *and his associate* MR
HENGLER, *and passing – as it were – down the High St towards the
White Hart Inn, where many* FORDINGTON RESIDENTS *wait to
greet it, before it turns off towards Salisbury Fields. The* CROWD
includes many we have already met, with the exception of the
MOULES *and* SARAH ELDRIDGE, *and those who we will discover
in Act Two to be presently at the Agricultural Dinner. The*
PROCESSION *is headed by* RIDERS *representing the* OMAR
PASHA, *a* BRITISH OFFICER, *a* FRENCH OFFICER, *a*
RUSSIAN PRINCE, *and a* GERMAN MERCENARY.

HENGLER. See! See the noble Omar Pasha, Supreme Commander
  of the Turkish Force in the Crimea!

MACARTE. Observe as well those brave young Englishmen in the
  service of the Turkish cause!

HENGLER. Not to mention our heroic Gallic allies!

MACARTE. Attend as well to the enemy, Prince Gorchakov:

HENGLER. and the pitiless and cruel Prussian mercenary General
  Luders.

MACARTE. View the might of men and armour of the Imperial
  Guard, the Volkynia Regiment and the dreaded Georgian
  Cossacks!

Meanwhile, the CROWD:

CROWD. Look, they're a-coming!
       Is that they?
       D'ye hear the band?
       Mama, what's a Gallic ally?
       Is that the Russians?
       No, that's a Turk.
       Hooray for Turkey!
       It's the Pasha!
       What's a Pasha?

And round about this point, the COMMENTARY *stops, and there
is* NARRATIVE:

NARRATIVE. And, near the White Hart,

> at the back of the crowd some people were aware
>
> of some old man,
>
> yes some old parson,
>
> who was shouting something it was hard to hear . . .
>
> *And* MOULE *is indeed there, trying to attract attention:*

MOULE. You must go home! You must leave this place!

NARRATIVE. But no one heard, or if they did, they ignored this odd old body –

MOULE. You must depart at once!

NARRATIVE. And so Henry Moule ran back towards the Green,

> trying to think of some way he could stop the growing flood of people as it swept towards his parish . . .
>
> *And now the* COMMENTARY *continues:*

HENGLER. Witness the Russian Army cross the River Pruth and advance into Moldavia!

MACARTE. Share plucky Turkey's heroic defence of Oltenitza against nine hundred thousand blood-hungry Muscovites!

HENGLER. And rejoice in fullest measure at the routing of the Slavic hordes at Giurgevo!

> *Meanwhile:*

CROWD. Boo! Shame!
>> Hooray!
>> Death to the Tsar!
>> Look at the Cossacks!
>> What a wonderful display!

The PROCESSION *reaches the thickest point of the* CROWD. *Suddenly,* MOULE *appears, on a strange, erratic steed. As the* NARRATIVE *describes events, the* CROWD *begins to boo and shout insults, throwing streamers and missiles, so* MOULE *is garlanded.*

NARRATIVE. And suddenly,

in the path of the procession,

appeared the strangest spectacle:

a parson, on a kind of horse or mule or pony that he couldn't well control,

and shouting warnings that could not be heard . . .

And when they recognised the man as the notorious killjoy Henry Moule,

the merry crowd,

particularly the younger set,

responded to this ludicrous performance with catcalls, boos and laughter,

and in some cases, even, missiles . . .

The catcalling and jeering reaches a crescendo. Then silence.

Until suddenly the crowd fell silent.

And each person asked their neighbour if they could make out

what the almost voiceless vicar had been shouting.

And like a fire the news spread through the huge assembly:

MOULE. I say – there is a stranger in our midst. His name is Cholera.

SOME. Cholera.

ALL. Cholera.

Blackout.

ACT TWO

Scene One

2.1.1. **The Fields near Fordington.** FANNY LOCK *lies there in the sun. The* FOOL *and the* LADY, *from a Plough Play, dance around her.*

FOOL. Come write me down the power above
        The man that first created love
        I'll give you gold, I'll give you pearl,
        If you can fancy me my girl.

LADY. It's not your gold should me entice
        Leave of virtue to follow your advice,
        But stay young man and you may find
        That this proud prim dame may prove more kind.

    The FOOL *and the* LADY *stay.* HORACE MOULE *has entered, with a spade and bag.*

HORACE. Well, so then, maidy. What's your name?

    FANNY *looks up.*

FANNY. Be Fanny. And what's it to you?

HORACE. And where d'you work then, Fanny?

FANNY. I'm in service, up in Dorchester.

HORACE. And who might you be serving?

FANNY. Mrs Eldridge, of the Dragon Brewery. You're full enough of who's and why's and where's. So who d'you be?

    Pause.

HORACE. My name's Horatio. Or – Horace. I'm the parson's son.

FANNY. Well well.

Slight pause.

So, Horatio or Horace. And what do we be doing, with our little bag and spade.

HORACE. We been a-digging for old pots and suchlike, with our little spade. And because it's thirsty work we've got a little bottle in our bag. And a bit of bread and cheese besides. And who knows, we might be looking out for somebody to share 'em.

FANNY. Oh, well. Might we now.

Long pause. Then FANNY *hops up, brushes herself down. As if that's settled.*

Well, what a summer, eh?

As they go off together.

FOOL. Now all my sorrows is come and past,
    For joy and bliss I've found at last . . .

LADY. So may all young ploughboys take their chance
    And lead their loves to the harvest dance:
    So lead me to the harvest dance.

NARRATORS *appear.*

NARRATIVE. For it was, and it had been, the most dazzling of summers,

and in the weeks before the harvest

they had strolled along the walks and through the fields,

had laid upon the beaches, run across the dunes and climbed the clifftops,

as if, like any dazzling summer, it would never end . . .

And suddenly, the FOOL *and the* LADY *take off their masks and speak to us.*

FOOL. And little knowing of the dread and deathly stranger who would come among them:

LADY. And little thinking of the poisoned seed so soon to sojourn in their midst.

2.1.2. **Fordington Vicarage.** *In the sudden darkness, a spot picks out a young man, dressed in black, and reading the Bible. It is* GEORGE MOULE.

GEORGE. And after this I looked, and behold, a throne was set in heaven, and one sat upon the throne. And round about the throne were four and twenty seats: and upon the seats I saw four and twenty elders sitting, clothed in white raiment:

Gradually, lights are growing around GEORGE; *we discover we are in the vicarage, at evening prayers, and with* GEORGE *are* MOULE, MRS MOULE, CHARLES, HANDLEY JNR, ELLEN WRIGHT *and the maid* HANNAH, *14.*

And out of the throne proceeded lightnings and thunderings and voices: and there were seven lamps of fire burning before the throne, which are the seven spirits of God.

GEORGE *closes the book.*

MOULE. Thank you. Now. Following our discussion of last evening, as to the nature of John's vision in this chapter of his Revelation, what further conclusions can we draw? George?

GEORGE. Well, father, does not the throne remind us of Jeremiah, and the 'glorious high throne' which 'from the beginning is the place of thy sanctuary'.

MOULE. Indeed. And – Charles?

CHARLES. We should note, father, should we not, that 'four and twenty elders' are prophesied as keepers of the Tabernacle in One Chronicles.

MOULE. Correct, and – Handley?

HANDLEY JNR. Um . . .

Pause.

GEORGE (*prompting*). The candlesticks . . .

HANDLEY JNR (*bit of a rush*). And are not the seven lamps of fire the seven candles of the self-same Tabernacle laid down in, Deuter –

MOULE. Exodus. So from all this we must conclude that the vision of St John is of the *actual* Holy Temple of Jerusalem.

Indeed, the scripture can admit no other interpretation. The question remains, however –

He stops, seeing HORACE *enter quickly with his bag. The rest of the* FAMILY *turn to identify the intruder.*

HORACE. Good evening. Sorry.

HANNAH. Mr *Horace.*

MOULE (*firmly*). – to which we shall address ourselves tomorrow. So, the Grace of Our Lord Jesus Christ, the Love of God, and the Fellowship of the Holy Spirit, be with us all for ever more.

ALL. Amen.

MOULE. Now Hannah, and you, Handley, time for bed.

HANNAH. Yes, sir.

HANDLEY JNR. Yes, father. Goodnight, mother.

Slight pause.

Horace.

He goes out after HANNAH.

GEORGE. I think . . . that Charles and I will work a little further on our presentation to the Annual Meeting of the Society for the Conversion of the Jews.

They go out, followed by ELLEN.

HORACE. I'm sorry.

MRS MOULE. We did wait.

HORACE. Thank you.

MOULE. Until we could do so no longer.

Pause. MRS MOULE *hands* HORACE *a letter.*

MRS MOULE. This came for you.

HORACE. Thank you, mother.

He opens the letter, and reads.

Oh, splendid.

MRS MOULE. Is it –

HORACE. They will take me at Queen's College, Cambridge, father.

MRS MOULE. Oh, that is excellent.

MOULE. Indeed. Particularly as he so singularly failed to graduate at Oxford.

Pause.

No doubt he will find Cambridge more congenial. Where he can happily surround himself with antinomians and universalists.

HORACE. I'm sorry. *Universal*ists?

MOULE. The heresy that all are ultimately graced, and that the immanence of sin and everlastingness of hell are morbid superstitions.

HORACE. Oh, I *see*. Well, there's an argument –

MOULE. What need has such an undemanding doctrine of the sustenance of prayer?

Pause.

HORACE. Father, I have been walking round your parish. The part down there. The iron foundry, Mill Street. Cuckold's Row. The area does not improve.

MOULE. No, it does not.

HORACE. But I suppose your argument would be that as they are so used to misery and torment in this life, they really won't mind if they're sentenced to the same in perpetuity.

MRS MOULE. Now, Horace, you must not –

HORACE. Because of course, it would be the rankest heresy even to consider the idea that paucity of spirit might be caused by poverty of circumstance –

MOULE. Oh, Horace.

His tone stops HORACE *in his tracks.*

Horace, I am full of fear. Fear and foreboding.

HORACE. Father, why?

MOULE. Because . . . Because John tells us there are seven
   angels, that are sent by God to pour the vials of his wrath upon
   the earth, and sea, and air. And for reason of man's disobedience
   and sin will sow upon the earth great plagues and pestilences.
   And who knows when the Day of Reaping will be come?

And in the distance, we hear the singing of a harvest hymn.

HARVESTERS. Hosanna say, hosanna sing,
                        The groaning harvest bring we in.
                        Hosanna sing, hosanna say,
                        For the harvest-home we make today.
                        Hosanna we sing, hosanna we say:
                        For the harvest-home we make today.

Scene Two

2.2.1. **The Dorchester Council.** *Again, suddenly, we switch to*
DARK MEN. *But then we realise it's only* NARRATORS *and*
TOWN COUNCILLORS, *the latter including* WILLIAM
HENNING, JOHN GALPIN, *41, the mayor* GEORGE
ANDREWS, *37, and* ALD. CHRISTOPHER ARDEN, *65.*

NARRATIVE. For in that very time, a meeting of the Corporation
   was assembled:

ARDEN. to consider the now overdue appointment,

HENNING. under the provisions of the Health of Towns Act,

ANDREWS. of an Inspector of Nuisances, Surveyor, Treasurer
   and Clerk.

NARRATIVE. Whereupon John Galpin,

HENNING. Town Councillor and Iron Foundry owner,

JOHN GALPIN. moved that these sanitary duties be combined,
   and the appointment put back till September.

NARRATIVE. While shortly after it was publicly announced that
   the Government intended to employ the Barracks,

GALPIN. now vacated by the military,

HENNING. as a depot for such inmates of the Millbank prison, London, as were pronounced free of the cholera which now rages there;

NARRATIVE. and that the Mayor George Andrews

ANDREWS. had immediately proceeded up to London to communicate the town's disquiet to the Secretary of State, but sadly was not fortunate enough to find Lord Palmerston in.

HENNING. Whereupon the Alderman and surgeon Dr Arden told the Council that he regretted the decision,

ARDEN. but would decline to sign a petition or memorial against it;

NARRATIVE. while Mr Galpin made it plain that in his view

JOHN GALPIN. all steps should now be taken to prevent, if possible, the infliction of this sanitary danger on the town.

2.2.2. **Mill Street.** RESIDENTS *sit round in the heat. They include* JANE SIBLEY, *now middle aged, and* MARTHA LOCK's *ten-year-old daughter* LOUISA. MOULE *stands a little apart. From off, a* WOMAN's *voice, loud. When we see her, we will recognise* LIZZIE SIBLEY, *now well into her 30s.*

LIZZIE SIBLEY (*off*). Hey, Martha! Martha Whiting! Just you bring that bonnet here!

JANE WHITING's *19-year-old daughter* MARTHA *runs on with a brightly-coloured hat.*

MARTHA. So why *you'm* wanting it? What use be she to you?

LIZZIE SIBLEY *runs in after* MARTHA.

LIZZIE SIBLEY. I said you fetch that here. Elsewise I fetch your mother to 'ee.

MARTHA *stops, shrugs.*

You wants to feather yoursen out, you learns to pay for it.

MARTHA *hands over the hat.*

MARTHA. Ah, well. There's some as needs their plumage more than t'others, bain't there, Mrs Sibley.

LIZZIE grabs the hat and goes, followed by MARTHA. MRS
LOCK *enters with a bucket from the mill stream.*

MARTHA LOCK. Why, good morning to you, parson.

She gives a cup of water from the bucket to LOUISA.

MOULE. Ah. Mrs Lock. And this I think – Maria?

MARTHA LOCK. No, Louisa. Twin. Maria's sick today.

MOULE. I'm sorry.

MARTHA LOCK. Oh, 'tin't uncommon. We bide that near the
mill stream, 'tis hard to keep a body spry.

MOULE. Well, no. And how's your eldest daughter –?

MARTHA. Fanny? Oh, she's in service, at the Eldridge brewery,
in Dorchester. But I doubt that meets with your approval,
parson.

MOULE. No.

MARTHA LOCK. But even so, maybe you do see, why I do
prefer our Fanny going up to Dorchester, like even to a brewer's
shop, than a-garnering the fruits of idleness round here.

From off, we hear the neigh of horses, and the voice of the publican,
GEORGE LODER.

GEORGE LODER. Gee up!

GEORGE LODER *drives in his dray, on which is piled dirty
washing. With him are* MR TURNLEY, *a prison warder, and
another,* YOUNG WARDER.

TURNLEY. So, this is it?

LODER. Should be.

To JANE:

Hey, you! This Florence Chaffley's house?

JANE (*shrugs*). Were yesterday.

LODER. Whoa there!

LODER *and the* WARDERS *dismount.*

LODER. Right. Florence! Florence Chaffley!

FLORENCE CHAFFLEY, *now 30, calls from within:*

FLORENCE (*off*). Ar! Who wants her?

LODER. 'Tis Mr –

TURNLEY. Turnley.

LODER. Mr Turnley with the washing. From the Barracks.

MOULE, *about to leave, turns back.* JANE *and* LIZZIE *look at each other with interest.* JANE *whispers to* LIZZIE, *who goes.*

FLORENCE (*off*). Oh, right, then. Be with you directly.

TURNLEY *looks at* JANE, *who smiles.* FLORENCE *emerges, tying on an apron.*

FLORENCE. Well, then. Good morning, Mr Turnley. Hello, George Loder. And how be trade with you?

LODER. Well, I has to say he's looking summat more cheerful than a-were.

FLORENCE. Well, that's a mercy. Right, then, Mr Turnley. We should be getting this lot back to you – I'd say, by Thursday, certainly.

TURNLEY. Uh, Wednesday would be better.

FLORENCE. See what I can do. Now come on, Janie Sibley, do you give us a hand.

JANE, FLORENCE *and the two* WARDERS *unload the washing.* MOULE *approaches.*

MOULE. Miss Chaffley. May I, may I ask what all this is?

Pause. FLORENCE *for some reason seems guilty.*

FLORENCE. Why, parson. Where d'you spring from?

Slight pause.

'Tis just washing.

They carry on unloading. During the following, LIZZIE SIBLEY *returns with* MARTHA WHITING, *who stands apart as* LIZZIE *goes and whispers to* TURNLEY. TURNLEY *then has a word with the* YOUNG WARDER, *who nods.*

JANE. Gennlemen's unmentionables.

FLORENCE. That's it.

JANE. Or p'raps in this case, mind, more *ungennlemen's* unmentionables.

FLORENCE. Well, yes.

JANE. Seeing as how they be locked up in the Barracks, like, for all kinds of most ungennlemanly behaviour.

MOULE. What, you mean, the convicts –?

FLORENCE. Yes. Well, that be around the length of it. But that don't mean their small-clothes don't get soiled, now do it? So let's have all this done.

FLORENCE carries on working.

TURNLEY. In fact, ma'am, I think we're going to have a draught of summat with this lady. On account of this uncommon heat.

FLORENCE. Well, there's nothing untoward in that.

TURNLEY. We'll be back in 20 minutes.

LIZZIE SIBLEY. Say an hour.

TURNLEY. An hour, then.

JANE (*leaving the washing*). Don't look like rain to me.

FLORENCE and LODER share a glance, as TURNLEY and the YOUNG WARDER follow out LIZZIE and JANE, joined by MARTHA, to the door of JANE WHITING's house, where that lady appears to greet them. We see that MARTHA LOCK has returned and is watching MOULE.

JANE WHITING. So in you do come, please, gentlemen. For a mug of summat, if you can be tempted in that way.

TURNLEY. Well, thank you, ma'am. A pleasure.

They are about to go in when JANE WHITING spots MOULE.

JANE WHITING. Well, if 'tisn't parson. Be it warm enough for 'ee?

MOULE. Yes, thank you. But I must, must warn you that there is a real risk –

JANE WHITING. Hey, parson. Do you ever meet my daughter Martha? Go on, Martha. Pay respects to Mr Moule.

MARTHA *curtsies, suggestively. All the* WOMEN *laugh. As they turn to go in.*

MOULE. 'And the heathen are sunk down into the cess-pit they have dug; and by the work of his own hands the wicked man is snared.'

EVERYONE *laughs again. The* SIBLEYS *start to sing – a mocking version of the old children's round song, but to the tune of the harvest song.*

SIBLEY SISTERS. Oh hokey, pokey, winky, wum
How do you like your taters done
Why all to pieces that's the fun
And can ye now just gie I one?

2.2.3. **Cornhill, Dorchester.** *Dorchester* CITIZENS – *who could include* MR PATCH *and* ANN BESANT – *formed to echo the previous Council* NARRATIVE.

NARRATIVE. And within a day or two, it was reported in the *County Chronicle,*

that the alarm created in the town by the arrival of the convicts had to a large degree subsided;

that the prospect of the Grand Equestrian Spectacular was now exciting the most keen anticipation, and

that following a harvest of the most munificent proportions,

the Annual Dinner of the Dorset Agricultural Society was set to be provided,

at the Antelope Hotel,

at five o'clock today.

2.2.4. **St George's Church, Fordington.** MOULE *is setting out fruit and vegetables for the harvest thanksgiving service.* AUGUSTUS HANDLEY *has entered.*

HANDLEY. Loder. George Loder. Publican.

MOULE. I think so. Yes.

HANDLEY. He'd lent his dray. Or – hired it, I'd imagine, for the washing.

MOULE. There was certainly a dray. What's happened, then, Augustus?

HANDLEY. He has developed colic. Headache. A little diarrhoea. As yet.

Pause.

MOULE. I see.

The crash of the church door.

Now, what on earth –

JANE WHITING *runs in.*

JANE WHITING. Parson! Where's parson?

MOULE. Mrs – Whiting?

JANE WHITING. There! There he be. The murderer! Assassin!

HANDLEY. Mrs Whiting, what is this?

JANE WHITING *starts attacking the harvest display.*

JANE WHITING. He puts a spell on her. 'Cos she do show lewd to he. And he do curse her with his talk of pits and snares and wickedness, and now she be dead –

HANDLEY *is trying to restrain her.*

HANDLEY. Please – please calm down . . .

JANE WHITING. Why he – why he –

HANDLEY. Your daughter's dead?

MOULE. Mrs Whiting, please –

JANE WHITING. Course. Course she be. First she'm all tired. Then her voice be hoarse. Now she do plim up like a bladder, and water stuff do come out of her, all yellow, and her nose do go pointy and her chin all blue . . . and she smell like – like I cass'n say . . .

HANDLEY. There is no question, I'm afraid –

Enter CHARLES *and* HANDLEY JNR. *They see the fruit and vegetables flung around.*

CHARLES. Father, what is this?

JANE WHITING *has begun to cry.*

JANE WHITING. Baa. Baa baa.

HANDLEY. The symptoms, undeniably –

MOULE *hears something:*

MOULE. What's that?

HANDLEY. First Loder. Now this woman's child –

JANE WHITING. Baa. Baa. You be . . .

MOULE. That noise – What is that noise?

HANDLEY JNR. It's music. It's the band. With the Equestrian parade.

MOULE. Parade?

JANE WHITING (*whimpering to herself*). Baa baa. You be the parson's lambs you be.

And now at last the harvest-home appears before us, a magnificent tableau of LABOURERS *and* FARMERS, *their sheaves of produce held before them, and the* CHILD *of the Harvest held aloft:*

HARVESTERS. So pray God's bounty never shall cease,
　　　　　　His providence shall e'er increase.
　　　　　　See what a burden bring we home,
　　　　　　When our next reaping shall be done –
　　　　　　What hosanna hear, what hosanna see:
　　　　　　When the harvest comes that is yet to be.

And suddenly the tableau splits, and we see the DIGNITARIES *of the Agricultural Dinner set behind.*

Scene Three

2.3.1. **The Antelope Hotel:** *The Agricultural Society Dinner. In the chair is* HENRY FRAMPTON, *with* WILLIAM HENNING *and the Mayor* GEORGE ANDREWS, *secretary of the Society, at his side.* DINERS *include* JOHN GALPIN. *There are also a number of* LABOURERS *and* SERVANTS *waiting to receive prizes, including* BENJAMIN VOSS, *a manservant,* SARAH HOLLAND, *a maidservant, and* JOHN LOCK. FRAMPTON *speaks:*

FRAMPTON. For gentlemen it is of course a privilege in any year to chair the Annual Meeting of this great Society –

Applause.

But it is so more than ever this year, when almighty providence has so particularly blessed us –

Applause.

And it thus becomes a more than usual honour to hand over to our most distinguished secretary, Mr Andrews, Mayor of Dorchester –

Applause.

– to announce the names of the recipients of the awards and premiums traditionally associated with this time.

ANDREWS. Mr Chairman. Gentlemen. The first premium goes to the manservant of a member or his widow, who shall have lived for the greatest number of years in one service, and who has retained good character. To Benjamin Voss, servant to Dr Christopher Arden £2.

VOSS *comes up for his prize.*

FRAMPTON. Well done, Voss. Very well done.

VOSS. Thank 'ee, sir.

ANDREWS. Second, to the domestic servant of a member who has lived the greatest number of years in one service, and whom if married has brought up her family in a respectable manner, £2 to Sarah Holland, servant to G.J. Andrews.

Laughter along with the applause as SARAH HOLLAND *receives her award.*

FRAMPTON. You're a lucky woman in your service, Holland. Well done.

ANDREWS. Well done, Sarah.

SARAH HOLLAND. Oh thank 'ee, sir. I be highly honoured, sir.

ANDREWS. And third, to the labourer in husbandry, who shall have brought up and maintained the greatest number of legitimate children, with the least proportion of parochial relief, £2 to John Lock, recommended by Captain Henning.

JOHN LOCK goes up for his envelope, to applause.

FRAMPTON. Well done then, Lock.

JOHN LOCK. Well, I be most grateful to you sir.

ANDREWS. And to the shepherd, who has reared the greatest number –

Suddenly, events are interrupted by the blowing of a horn. It's NATTY SEALE.

FRAMPTON. What's this? What do you want?

NATTY. This be old Natty Seale, this be. Who'm right sorry to be interrupting, like. But so's not to put too sharp an end on things, there be cholera broke out in Fordington.

Staggered silence.

All part of providence's bounty, gentlemen.

The dinner splits up with remarkable speed. JOHN LOCK *stands amid it all with his envelope.* HENNING *comes to* NATTY.

HENNING. Seale.

NATTY. Ay, sir?

HENNING. How did you learn this dreadful news?

NATTY. Why, from the parson, sir. Rode up on some old ramshackle animal, in front of the equestrian procession. Di'n't half look a silly sammel, mind. But when he do say cholera, they do hear'n then. That's sure as sure.

GALPIN is hurrying past.

HENNING. Galpin.

JOHN GALPIN. Yes, Captain Henning?

HENNING. Look. You know Moule.

JOHN GALPIN. Of course. Most of my foundryhands are his parishioners. Not that's he's very popular.

HENNING. I know. But he has this, this vast family . . . And between us, we could accommodate them away from the worst of it. At least until the worst is over. As an act of, Christian . . .

Pause.

JOHN GALPIN. You mean, as a good work, Captain Henning.

HENNING. Well, I wouldn't actually, if I were you, I wouldn't mention good works, Mr Galpin.

2.3.2 The Vicarage, Fordington. *Open chests stand in the room.* GEORGE, CHARLES, *and* HANDLEY JNR *are bringing in piles of clothes and dumping them in the chests, assisted by* HANNAH *and* ELLEN WRIGHT. MRS MOULE *is bringing in bottles of liquids and putting them on a table. Everything is very busy.*

MRS MOULE. Charles, have you been through all the servants' linen?

CHARLES. Yes, mother.

MRS MOULE. George, we must pack up all the winter underwear . . . Where's Hannah?

HANNAH. Here, ma'am.

MRS MOULE. Please help Mr Charles.

MOULE *has entered with* HENNING, ANN HENNING *and* JOHN GALPIN. *The business continues with the* SONS *coming in and out with more clothes, as the conversation progresses.*

HENNING. Mr Moule, I appreciate that we have not seen eye to eye. But this is an offer from our hearts. We have our coach, and Mr Galpin's cabriolet outside. You are *all* most welcome to come with us.

HANDLEY JNR. I've looked in the back attic, mother. Nothing.

MOULE. I am of course most grateful for your offer –

ANN HENNING. Mr Moule. In times like these, disputes, misunderstandings, surely fade away and we can see each other as we are, God's creatures –

GEORGE. Mama, I can't find the winter clothes!

MOULE. But I'm afraid I cannot –

MRS MOULE. Back hall closet!

JOHN GALPIN. Look, reverend. Let's not beat about the bush. You have a country parson's living. There are – what, ten people here? Where are you going? Where will you be accommodated?

MRS MOULE. There must be more shirts somewhere, Charles.

MOULE. Going? I am going nowhere.

HENNING. Sorry?

MOULE. That is what I have been trying to explain. My parish has been struck by cholera. My place is here.

ANN HENNING. You mean – you mean to stay?

MOULE. That is my meaning quite precisely.

JOHN GALPIN (*pointing at the baggage*). So what's all this?

MOULE. These are the garments of this household we can spare, to clothe those whose own raiment is infected by the pestilence.

JOHN GALPIN. But surely, Mr Moule, your wife, your children and your staff –

MOULE. Mary, would you like to accept this kind offer, from this lady and these gentlemen?

MRS MOULE. I thank them for it. But, no, I will stay here.

MOULE. And what is the view of our children?

MRS MOULE. They will stay.

MOULE. Have you asked our servants?

MRS MOULE. Yes. They too.

MOULE. Well, then. It does appear . . .

Pause.

HENNING. We have made our offer in good faith. There's nothing more to say.

He turns to go, followed by ANN HENNING. *But* JOHN GALPIN *has one last try.*

JOHN GALPIN. Look, Moule. There's something that you ought to know.

MOULE. What's that?

JOHN GALPIN. I've been talking to a fellow at the barracks. And he says, in London, nobody is safe.

MOULE. I'm sorry?

JOHN GALPIN. Don't you understand? It isn't like before. It's not just in the slums, among the feckless and the miserable. It's taking tradesmen. And professional people. Gentry, even.

MOULE. Well, in that case, Mr Galpin, you must pray our efforts to restrict its spread succeed. Or otherwise, who knows who might be stricken.

Pause. ANN HENNING *runs out.*

JOHN GALPIN. Well. Have it your way, reverend.

He turns and goes, followed by HENNING.

MRS MOULE. We are well provided with the chlorides and the aromatics. We must take care however not to run out of laudanum. And –

MOULE. Indeed. George! Handley!

Enter GEORGE *followed by* HANDLEY JNR.

GEORGE. Father?

Re-enter ANN HENNING *with a bag of clothes. She puts it on the table with the others.*

ANN HENNING. For your – parishioners.

She's going, as MOULE *looks in the bag.*

MOULE. But, madam . . . these are silks, brocades . . .

ANN HENNING. Mr Moule, you will not make us guilty. You will not.

She goes out.

MOULE. We must take the kitchen copper set to Mill Street. Augustus is already there. We must get a fire going, boil the victims' clothes. Except the ones we need to burn.

The SONS *go.* MOULE *follows.* MRS MOULE, *alone, falls to her knees. Very intense, very fast, very pained:*

MRS MOULE. Oh Lord I thank Thee that in judgement Thou dost thus remember mercy. Keep me ready for Thy call should it please Thee to take me to Thyself by this fearful disease. It makes the flesh terrible; fix mine eyes on Jesus and it shall have no terror . . .

A MUMMER *appears.*

MUMMER. So in come I Beelzebub
             On my shoulder I carries a club
             In my hand a dripping-pan,
             Don't you think I'm a funny old man?

2.3.3. **The Dragon Brewery.** SARAH *enters, followed by* EMILY, SARAH ALBINIA *and* SOPHIE.

EMILY. Mama, why not?

SARAH. Why not? Is this a brewerey?

SARAH ALBINIA. But just to *Weymouth.* For a *week.*

SARAH. Then why don't you go with your sister.

SARAH ALBINIA. Oh, mama . . .

SARAH. But I – I will not go.

Slight pause.

EMILY. Then I won't either.

SARAH. We'll all stay.

Slight pause.

For it won't spread. For 'tis a – a disease of – the afflicted. The already wretched, sickly and debased.

She catches SOPHIE's *eye, then turns to* EMILY.

It will not touch us, Emily.

Scene Four

2.4.1. **Mill Street**. REV HANDLEY, GEORGE *and* CHARLES *working round a copper, boiling over a fire.* FORDINGTON PEOPLE *bring them clothes in wheelbarrows; they put them in the copper and boil them, then remove them and lay them out. A group of* CHILDREN *play nearby. They're singing:*

CHILDREN.   Eena meena mino mo
                  Kewska leena lina lo
                  Eggs butter cheese and bread
                  Stick stock stone dead
                  And out goes SHE.

2.4.2. **The Locks' House**. MARTHA LOCK *is almost hysterical.* MOULE *is with her. Little* LOUISA *stands by the door, distressed by her mother's state.*

MOULE. Now, Mrs Lock, please, let us make rice water . . .

MARTHA LOCK. Oh, sir, oh, Mr Moule, just the sight of him, I cass'n –

MOULE. Now, why not sit down, for a moment, why –

MARTHA LOCK. I mean, the colour o f's face, the stuff comes out of en –

MOULE. Just for a moment, so you can –

MARTHA LOCK. See, 'tis not like anything I d'ever see. 'Tis like a – flood, a bursting blather. I could never fancy so much do come out of one frame so fast. And I cass'n touch 'en.

Slight pause.

That's what 'tis. For all them years, I held 'en. Now he'm a-dying. And I cass'n bear to touch my son.

MOULE. Mrs Lock. You will not have to for too long.

MARTHA LOCK (*crying*). But even so . . .

    MOULE *nods to* LOUISA, *who goes out.*

MOULE. Now, ma'am, where is your husband?

MARTHA LOCK. In the fields.

MOULE. Can he be sent for?

MARTHA LOCK. Sent for? No.

MOULE. Why not? Your little girl . . .

MARTHA LOCK (*obvious*). He be a-working, sir.

MOULE. But – but –

MARTHA LOCK. I mean, he cassn'n afford to take a holiday. If so be Henry . . . still we've seven mouths to feed. He be able bodied; like Parish don't give him no relief.

MOULE. Mrs Lock. Did you say that you have *seven* of your family living here?

MARTHA LOCK. That's it. Since our Fanny went to service. Like, we eat and live in here, this room, while we do sleep in t'other.

Enter FANNY LOCK *in her maid's uniform. She's covered in ordure, her face white.*

FANNY LOCK. Mother. He be gone.

A pause. MARTHA LOCK *looks at* MOULE.

MARTHA LOCK. So. D'you keep a Bible 'bout you, Mr Moule?

MOULE. Why, yes, indeed . . .

He finds his Bible *and hands it to her. She opens it arbitrarily, and hands it back.*

MARTHA LOCK. Then find me consolation.

A MUMMER *appears.*

MUMMER. Here come I old Poor and Mean
         Hardly worthy to be seen,
         Half be starved and t'other half blind
         With a well-ricked back and a broken mind

2.4.3. **The Dragon Brewery.** SARAH, EMILY, SOPHIE *and* SARAH ALBINIA. SARAH *is busy on her accounts.*

SARAH. So. Do we hear a word from Fanny?

SARAH ALBINIA. No mama. Not since she's gone.

EMILY. What, Fanny gone? Whatever for?

SOPHIE. Because her family lives in Mill Street. So she's gone back.

EMILY. But isn't that –

SOPHIE. In case they are struck down. In case they are infected by this dreadful sickness, and they need her.

SARAH looks quickly at her step-daughter. SOPHIE looks firmly back. A moment.

SARAH ALBINIA. They say they've got the farmers to let loose the hatches.

SARAH. What?

EMILY. To flood the meadows, sluice the, you know, from the land.

SARAH. Sounds sensible.

SOPHIE. And he – and they, his sons, are working in the most afflicted streets. To boil and disinfect the clothing. In their kitchen copper.

SARAH. Are they now.

Pause. SARAH works on. Then.

SARAH. Oh – don't – you – *dare.*

And away, we can hear the cry of GEORGE and HORACE as they ride through the farmers' fields:

GEORGE. Farmers! Open your locks! Let forth the waters!

HORACE. Raise your hatches! Farmers! Open your locks!

And we hear the CHILDREN singing.

CHILDREN. Hokey pokey wangery tum
            Plokery, hockery, bulum, kum
            Wingery, fungery, wingery wum
            King of the Cannibal Islands . . .

2.4.4. The Fudge Home. EDWARD FUDGE, *now 41, his father* WILLIAM, *now 69, kneeling beside his dead wife* SUZANNAH. MOULE *is there.*

EDWARD FUDGE. Well, parson. D'you see, I got meself a family.

MOULE. Mr Fudge, in this your time of desperate grief –

EDWARD FUDGE. And I scrimp and save and p'raps I starve a bit, to keep father and mother in their last years.

MOULE. Mr Fudge, I pray, you must not –

EDWARD FUDGE. And now we be rewarded for our husbandry. My Ann, my Johnathan. Now my mother, his Suzannah. So do you reckon, that's our just deserving?

MOULE. Edward. Please tell me, why you came here, to this place.

EDWARD FUDGE. Oh, that. That's easy. Being as how my father caught pneumonia one winter, and squire squot his house. And being as I tells squire he should leave poor father in his place, there bain't no work for I. So we ups, like all of us. And we comes here, to Mill Street. Is that your answer, Mr Moule?

Pause.

MOULE. I can – I have – there's nothing I can say.

He goes upstage to WILLIAM FUDGE. *But* EDWARD, *insistent, grabs him by the shoulder.*

EDWARD FUDGE. And maybe now at last you'm sorry for what you do say to en?

Enter CHARLES MOULE.

CHARLES (*breathless*). Ah. Father. Mr Handley asks: can you call on Mrs Sibley. Jane. In Ansty Street.

MOULE *prepares to go.*

MOULE. Yes. Yes, of course. What's that?

He's hearing the CHILDREN *singing.*

CHARLES. It's children. Singing plague-songs. From the Middle Ages. 'Out goes she.'

Slight pause.

MOULE. They hear the beatings of the wings of Azrael.

CHARLES. Azrael?

MOULE. Death's angel. Who lurks unseen in every open privy. Every drain. But who need not. And who *should* not, in a country groaning with the bounty of God's providence and plenty . . .

Pause.

And the Corporation tells me they can find me no more laudanum. And that they cannot find me three – or even *one*, more copper for the clothes.

Pause.

But I am informed that they will close the *pigsties*.

He looks into the eyes of EDWARD FUDGE.

CHILDREN. One a zoll, zen a zoll
          Zig a zoll zan
          Bobtail vinegar tittle toll tan
          Harum Scarum Virgin Marum
          YOU

2.4.5 **The Sibley Home, Ansty Street.** LIZZIE SIBLEY *with her child* ALBERT, *ten, and a crib.* MOULE *appears from an inner room.*

MOULE. Well, I'm afraid your sister's dead.

LIZZIE SIBLEY. Um, do she –

MOULE. No. She did not regain consciousness. She did not repent her of her sin, before the end. I'm sorry.

LIZZIE *doesn't want him to go.*

LIZZIE SIBLEY. Parson.

MOULE. Yes, Mrs –

LIZZIE SIBLEY. Miss, if I be honest, parson.

MOULE. Yes. I see.

Slight pause.

LIZZIE SIBLEY. Parson, us used – that's Jane and me, oh, twenty years back, us did shout and us did bawl at you. Athwart the Lych Gate. And I do very well mind your old maid a-shouting back: 'You be the devil's sheep you be'.

Pause.

And I guess now she be right. Don't you?

MOULE. Now, Mrs – Mrs –

LIZZIE SIBLEY. But still. Whatever she done. And whatever I done, cass'n deserve all this. Now can we?

Pause.

MOULE. Miss Sibley. I must tell you, it is my belief, that this dreadful sickness is a visitation of God's just and wrathful judgement on His sinful and forgetful children. For . . . as was said to me, by someone living in this very quarter: sin is an abomination, there is no excuse, and no reprieve. And its child is cursed for all eternity.

He turns and leaves quickly.

2.4.6. **Ansty Street.** MOULE *emerges into the street, and meets* MARTHA LOCK. *With her are* JOHN LOCK *and* FANNY. *Behind, in the gloom, another figure. It's* HORACE.

MARTHA LOCK. Well, Mr Moule. And here you be.

MOULE. Why, Mrs Lock, and – John. And – Horace?

HORACE. Yes. Yes, father, I –

MARTHA LOCK. And p'raps it's best if I explain.

Pause.

For it's about our Fanny, who's in service in the town, and we did have great hopes for. Well, not to beat around it, we do learn as she's been seeing this young gentleman, to whom we do hear you be related. And they just been a-telling us, as how there'll be another joining 'em. In a few months' time.

MOULE. I –

MARTHA LOCK. And they say that troubles never come, but they do come in regiments.

MOULE. I must –

MARTHA LOCK. And that 'the heathen are sunk down into the cess-pit they have dug'. Or so we do hear it whispered, Mr Moule.

Another figure emerges from the darkness. It's FLORENCE CHAFFLEY, carrying her possessions in a bundle.

FLORENCE. Well, if 'tisn't parson. Where d'you spring from, eh?

A thin, sick laugh.

The Reverend Moule. As the whole world knows. A-telling folks to change their ways. A-telling me. When I lose my third, at not yet seventeen. And change I do, mind. Be no more young soldiers, off behind the waxworks at the races. No. Takes up a decent trade, I do. And takes in washing.

Pause.

Washing.

Pause.

Don't I, eh?

MOULE *looks from* FLORENCE *to the* LOCKS *and his son. He closes his eyes. When he opens them, he sees little* FLORENCE CHAFFLEY, *with her tray.*

FLORENCE. Well, parson. Mushrooms? Firewood? Lemon balm?

MOULE *looks at* FLORENCE, *desperately, and then stumbles away.*

2.4.7. **The Streets of Fordington.** *Simultaneously,* CHILDREN *sing and four dark figures – who could but do not have to include* MOULE's *sons and* AUGUSTUS HANDLEY – *recite from four corners the most famous verses from the Book of Revelation; and* HENRY MOULE *mumbles words and phrases from Revelation, as he stumbles through the darkness, the* CHILDREN *dancing around him and, at the end of each verse, one falling dead.*

CHILDREN. Eena meena mino mo
         Kewska leena lina lo
         Eggs butter cheese and bread
         Stick stock stone dead
         And out goes SHE.

FIRST FIGURE. 'And behold when the Lamb opened one of the seals and I heard, as it were the noise of thunder, one of the four beasts saying, Come and see. And I saw, and behold a white horse: and he that sat on him had a bow; and a crown was given unto him: and he went forth conquering, and to conquer.'

MOULE (*after '. . . Come and see'*). And the seven angels said come hither . . .

SECOND FIGURE. 'And when he had opened the second seal, I heard the second beast say, Come and see. And there went out another horse that was red; and power was given to him that sat thereon to take peace from the earth, and that they should kill one another; and there was given unto him a great sword.'

MOULE (*after '. . . Come and see'*). And I saw the great whore . . . that sitteth upon many, many waters . . .

THIRD FIGURE. 'And when he had opened the third seal, I heard the third beast say, Come and see. And I beheld, and lo a black horse; and he that sat on him had a pair of balances in his hand. And I heard a voice in the midst of the four beasts say, A measure of wheat for a penny, and three measures of barley for a penny, and see thou hurts not the oil and the wine.'

MOULE (*after '. . . Come and see'*). . . . and I saw a dragon with great horns . . .

FOURTH FIGURE. 'And when he had opened the fourth seal, I heard the voice of the fourth beast say, Come and see. And I looked and behold a pale horse; and his name that sat on him was Death.'

THIRD FIGURE. Was Death.

SECOND FIGURE. Was Death.

FIRST FIGURE. Was Death.

MOULE. . . . and the dragon stood before the woman, to devour her child as soon as it was born . . .

And suddenly there is silence everywhere, and all focus shifts to HENRY MOULE, *kneeling over the body of the last, dead* CHILD. *Then he looks up into darkness around him and before him, and sees.*

MOULE. Who are you?

Pause.

Where do you come from? Why are you here?

Pause.

WHO ARE YOU?

Long pause. And perhaps we, too, see something like three white ANGELS, *surrounding some kind of huge, smoking vessel, appear and disappear.*

Saw. Three angels. Saw. Three strangers. And I John . . . saw the Holy City. New Jerusalem. And behold I make all things new.

Suddenly, MOULE *is aware of something wet falling on his upturned face.*

It's – *rain . . .*

2.4.8. **The Vicarage.** *At first, we see just* ALD. ARDEN. *Then gentle lights fade up in the Vicarage where* MRS MOULE *reads* ARDEN's *letter.* HANDLEY *is there, working with a ledger, and* HORACE *standing to the side.*

ARDEN. So, Mr Moule. On Saturday four died. On Sunday three. Today but two. And I have to tell you, there has not been a single case in Dorchester. And with the change in weather, in my judgement, now, there will not be. Thanks be to God.

MRS MOULE *(folding the letter).* Amen.

HANDLEY. So. Thirty. Inclusive of four infants and six children under ten. Beginning with George Loder, publican. And ending with Elizabeth Sibley, seamstress. Seamstress and prostitute.

MOULE *enters. He still looks dishevelled.*

HORACE. Father –

MOULE. Mary, please find me Hebrews.

MRS MOULE. Henry, you were supposed to rest.

But she goes to find the Bible.

MOULE. For you see, methought I saw . . . the copper, but I did not see my friend Augustus, and the copper was not as mine is small but nigh unto the height of men . . . And there was not one but three . . . Mary, find, Hebrews, thirteen, please . . .

MRS MOULE. Of course.

She finds the chapter and reads.

'Let brotherly love continue. Be not forgetful to entertain strangers; for thereby some have entertained angels unawares. Remember them that are in bonds, as bound with them, and them which suffer –'

MOULE. Yes. Yes. I saw them. Saw the angels. Yes.

He takes the Bible and reads to himself.

HORACE. Father.

MOULE *turns to* HORACE.

Father, we must speak about this child. We must speak about this – Fanny. Because, you see, despite her station –

MRS MOULE. Horace, please. Not now.

Pause.

HANDLEY. 'And the heathen are sunk down into the cess-pit they have dug. And by the work of his own hands the wicked man is snared.'

MOULE. But . . . shall the needy always be forgotten? Must their expectations perish?

Slight pause.

When there is no need?

He looks at HORACE. *Suddenly bitter, throwing* HORACE's *own words back at him:*

But you. What misery? What poverty of circumstance?

He turns quickly and goes.

MRS MOULE. Well, yes. Well, yes, indeed.

She stands and moves a little apart. HANDLEY *turns to* HORACE *and tries to explain:*

HANDLEY. She will – of course they will both be provided for. The father – Lock – he has been spoken to. Arrangements have been made.

MRS MOULE (*from the doorway*). Oh, Horace. Why couldn't she and you have been the phantoms? and his blessed angels real?

Scene Five

2.5.1. **The Dragon Brewery.** *In the yard, and the parlour. In the parlour,* JOHN JAMES BESANT *sits and waits. In the yard,* SARAH, SOPHIE, EMILY, SARAH ALBINIA *and* ALFRED MASON. *They are in the middle of a considerable argument.*

SARAH. Well, I really can't imagine what I'm supposed to say.

EMILY. Now, mother, surely it's not necessary to say anything at all.

ALFRED. And isn't it in everybody's best interests –

SARAH. Not necessary? What, 'Good morning, gentlemen, I'm so sorry to have troubled you –'

EMILY. And *I* really can't imagine why you had them sent for in the first place.

SARAH. Oh, you can't? Why, with their loved ones off and disappeared, without the slightest hint of where you'd gone or when you'd be returned, with your beds unslept in, little Katherine and Charles abandoned –

SARAH ALBINIA. Oh, mama!

EMILY. They are in Weymouth. With their nurse. And Sophie's –

SARAH. And I must say that it ill becomes you, Emily, as the only one I'd ever thought to be approximately sensible, I must say your involvement in this business is the greatest shock to me.

EMILY (*with a look to* SOPHIE). I was talked into it.

SARAH. And you married to a Borough Councillor besides.

SARAH ALBINIA. Now, please, mama –

SARAH. And that's not to say, young Sarah, that you are absolved, for all your 'oh' and 'please mamas'. I always been afeared you could be easy led astray, and fall into bad influence, and see now, I was right.

ALFRED. Now, Sarah, surely –

SARAH. And I'll thank you Alfred to refrain from surelying and telling me what's in my interests, because –

Enter CHRISTIAN. *During this,* JOHN TIZARD *joins* JOHN JAMES BESANT *in the parlour.*

CHRISTIAN. Uh – ma'am. It's Miss, Miss Emily's –

SARAH. Now, see. The Councillor's arrived.

CHRISTIAN. And, um, Miss Sophie's – Mr John James, I do put him in the parlour, like as well.

SARAH. Well, then.

She looks fiercely at her daughters. EMILY *makes the first move into the parlour, followed by* SOPHIE *and* SARAH ALBINIA. *We see* JOHN TIZARD *and* JOHN JAMES BESANT *hurry to greet their wives and ask after them as, still in the yard,* SARAH *turns on* ALFRED.

SARAH. I mean. To give them free run of the brewery. I mean, to let them take the dray. I can't think what possessed you, Alfred.

Pause.

ALFRED. Sarah. She is your daughter.

SARAH. Well now, Alfred, that's not strictly so, and I must confess there's times, and this be one of them –

ALFRED. And just imagine, Sarah, standing up to you.

Slight pause.

SARAH. Well, I can't think what you mean.

ALFRED. Oh yes, you can.

ALFRED *gestures* SARAH *towards the parlour.* SARAH *allows herself to be gestured in. As she and* ALFRED *enter:*

JOHN TIZARD. Well, she must have summoned us for *something.*

JOHN JAMES. I'd been on the road two hours –

SARAH *and* ALFRED *have arrived.*

SARAH. Ah, John. How goes the partnership?

JOHN TIZARD. Well, excellently, thank you, mother-in-law –

SARAH. And the corporation? Be the streets of Weymouth lit and clean?

JOHN TIZARD. Well, moderately, on last acquaintance, yes, but –

SARAH. And John James? You were found?

JOHN JAMES. Yes. I was on my way to Salisbury.

SARAH. In pursuit of some arcane scholastic interest, no doubt.

JOHN TIZARD. And now perhaps you will explain –

JOHN JAMES. Well, yes, indeed –

SARAH. Oh, it's quite simple, John, John James. Last night, my daughters took it to themselves to borrow – well, one might say, to appropriate a dray, a pair of horses and a vital item of equipment from the brewery –

JOHN JAMES. What's that?

SARAH ALBINIA. T'was our old copper.

SARAH. *My* old copper, which they'd this notion to take down to Fordington –

JOHN TIZARD. To *Fordington?*

SARAH. That's it.

JOHN JAMES. What, where the cholera –

SARAH. Muscular Christianity, I'm told it do be called.

   JOHN TIZARD *is looking at* EMILY.

EMILY. Don't look at me.

SARAH. And all because –

SOPHIE. Because we did think that they might have need of it. Because we thought that we might help, down there. That's all.
   Pause.

JOHN TIZARD. Well, Emily, I – don't know what to say.
   Pause.

EMILY. She wouldn't come. I wanted her to come to Weymouth. And then none of this . . .

Pause.

JOHN JAMES. Well, I suppose, as Virgil has it in the *Georgics*, '*Semper hoc* –'

SARAH *can stay silent no longer.*

SARAH. And so who d'you think you are? St George? Some great saviour of all mankind, a-charging round the countryside, a-rescuing everyone and everything?

SOPHIE. And who are you, mama? Are you the dragon, snapping and a-snarling round your gates, to keep out anything and anybody you don't know?

SARAH. I mean, did you think once, just once, mind, did you remember *for one moment* that you be a mother, with two children, and if you'd not come back –

SOPHIE. Oh, mama, can you think for a moment it might be *because.*

Pause.

SARAH. Well, no. Maybe I can't.

Slight pause.

Maybe because I see it t'other way.

Slight pause.

Like, folks with so much love for everyone, and everything, and everybody, that they've none left over for their own.

She takes out a letter. She hands it to SOPHIE.

Like your – your blessed Reverend Moule.

SOPHIE *reads the letter. Then she hands it to* EMILY.

JOHN TIZARD. What is it?

EMILY. It's – it's a letter, from our maid.

2.5.2. **The Dragon and elsewhere.** *As* EMILY *reads, we see* FANNY, *with a suitcase, near a* DEAD MUMMER *on the ground. Another* MUMMER *kneels beside.*

FANNY. And so, ma'am, it do be concluded, by my father and the parson, it be better for all parties if I go off on a boat, and has my baby in Australia.

And I'm sorry that I cass'n tell you properly. But it all fall out so fast. And Christian said she'd write it down for me. And let you know.

CHRISTIAN *appears.*

CHRISTIAN. And it do seem a long way. I'll be quite honest, ma'am. It do seem far. It do seem far, to have a baby.

The mourning MUMMER *delivers the lament.*

MUMMER. For of children eleven I've got but seven,
        And they be started up to heaven.
        Out of the seven I've got but five,
        And they be starved to death alive.
        Out of the five I've got but three,
        And they be popped behind a tree;
        Out of the three there is but one:
        And he got round behind the sun.

SARAH, *to* SOPHIE, *but gesturing towards Fordington:*

SARAH. So who d'you think you are, St George?

Scene Six

2.6.1. **Outside the Vicarage, Fordington.** MOULE *appears, takes* MRS MOULE's *arm. They leave their house, to walk into Dorchester.* NATTY SEALE *and the geriatric* CAROLINE *await them.*

NATTY. Well, morning, parson. You and missus off to pick up your testimonial, like?

MOULE. Yes, that's right, Mr Seale.

NATTY. Be enough red faces up at Town Hall, I do venture. Like, to see you honoured and hosanna'd and all that . . .

MRS MOULE. Yes. Yes, Mr Seale. I think there may well be.

2.6.2. **The Town Hall, Dorchester.** *Most of the leading citizens of the town are assembling, including* HENNING, ANN HENNING,

REV HANDLEY, MR PATCH, JOHN GALPIN, ANN
BESANT *and* SARAH ELDRIDGE's DAUGHTERS. *In the chair
is the mayor* GEORGE ANDREWS; *beside him sit* CAPT
HENNING *and* ALDERMAN ARDEN. *It is clear that none of
them are completely happy with the proceedings. The* MOULES *enter
and join them at the top table.*

ANDREWS. Ladies and gentlemen. It falls to me to open the
business of the meeting. Now, we have met here, as we are all
aware, to take part in one of the most pleasurable proceedings
that, as I think, a number of persons can be mixed up with.

That hasn't come out quite right, but he ploughs on.

We have met to testify your – approbation of the exertions and
self-denying conduct of a very excellent and estimable gentleman,
and an equally excellent and estimable lady. I feel myself most
inadequate to set before you the qualities of this lady and
gentleman . . .

Calls of 'shame'.

Indeed, when I read the list of the subscribers, I cannot think
but that I am a most unworthy person to be in this place at all!

Another, perhaps more muted, cry of 'shame'.

And so I hand the business over to my friend and colleague
Captain Henning with some considerable relief!

Slight pause.

Who will present the testimonial, on behalf of the subscribers.

ANDREWS *sits,* HENNING *stands.*

HENNING. Um – Mr Mayor. Ladies and gentlemen. It is my
pleasant task to acknowledge our – the feelings of deep gratitude
that must be felt by every honest citizen to, as you said, your
Worship, a most estimable gentleman and lady.

Any form of testimonial we can present must fall far short of
what they both deserve. They will assert no doubt they did their
duty. But how many were there to be found who did that?

Or who acknowledged, even, what that duty was. Or to whom it
should be, shown.

And I think that I should best discharge *my* duty, now, by presenting without further observation this testimonial to Mr and Mrs Moule, in the name of the subscribers.

He hands over a silver salver, and gestures to a small cabinet and set of clerical robes. He sits, relieved. MOULE *stands.* HENNING *has forgotten the third part of the testimonial, and has omitted to describe the gifts,* ANDREWS *whispers to him furiously and he has to leap straight up again.*

MOULE. My dear sir, my kind friends –

HENNING. The testimonial, in fact, consists –

MOULE *sits.*

– of a silver salver, of chaste design, inscribed, a set of clerical robes, and a Devonport cabinet, most handsomely fitted up, for Mrs Moule. And, the contribution being more than expected, a purse of . . .

He doesn't know the amount. ANDREWS *whispers.*

. . . of 170 sovereigns.

He sits. A smattering of slightly embarrassed applause. MOULE *stands again.*

MOULE. My dear sir, my kind friends, my fellow townsmen, I sincerely thank you. Did I stand here merely as a man, I should regard this as a proud occasion; but I stand here rather as a Christian minister, and feel bound to say that, had I acted under the influence of more natural feelings, I should not have stood here at all. To God be all the glory!

ANDREWS *and* HENNING *nod, and look relieved.*

As to the blame for the awfulness of this visitation, I have as you might surmise applied my mind, and I must tell you it is my belief that Fordington was not to blame – though one might speak of its vice and degradation, nor yet the county – though one should consider the responsibility of landowners who throw their tenants on the mercy of the urban parishes, nor even Dorchester and its borough corporation – though I must own that for the dereliction of its sanitary duties there are those who sit upon that corporation who should feel ashamed.

The odd look, but MOULE *continues:*

But even so, in my opinion, ladies, sirs, the blame lies in substantive part elsewhere: at the door of those who for the last sixty years have managed the estates of his Royal Highness Albert Duke of Cornwall.

Pause. An intake of breath.

For they, when they might have prevented it, allowed such a state of things to grow up, largely it is true on a piece of freehold land, but one surrounded on all sides by His Royal Highness' property, a property which consists moreover of two thousand acres of the finest soil in England, worked by labourers who live crushed into a space which cannot overreach five acres, and which has become a great sink into which the excremental filth of all the neighbouring parishes is poured.

This is getting near the bone.

In circumstances of such misery and squalor that such a visitation was inevitable. But, I have to say, in one respect at least, and by the simplest and the cheapest means of sanitary contrivance, nonetheless *avoidable.*

He looks round at the citizenry.

I have written I must tell you to Prince Albert to acquaint him with my views.

This provokes shock.

And I have been informed, as I well knew, that the Prince himself has no personal authority, and that the Duchy has no formal and thus will accept no moral responsibility for the state of Mill Street, Ansty Street and Cuckold's Row.

Complete silence.

To which, good citizens, I have already made reply. For I will not rest until this wrong is righted. For it is a species of oppression, and it will and should provoke resistance. And I say all this as one to whom, until these dreadful happenings occurred, such views as I now entertain were strangers.

Pause. He looks at the gifts.

So now, in my own name as well as that of my wife, all that remains to say is that we thank you, from the bottom of our hearts, for these kind testimonials.

Which we receive on behalf of all, those known to us and those unknown, who strove to keep this dreadful plague from spreading from my parish into yours.

He sits. ANDREWS *stands.*

ANDREWS. Well, now, perhaps . . . If any lady or gentleman would care to lead off with God Save the Queen, there could not, I think, be a more appropriate way of ending these proceedings. Mr Patch –?

To our and her own surprise, SARAH ALBINIA ELDRIDGE *has stood up.*

SARAH ALBINIA. Mr Mayor. You do not think it even more appropriate, to sing a hymn?

ANDREWS (*not sure, looking around*). Well, yes.

HENNING. Yes, certainly . . .

There is a quick debate among the ELDRIDGE *sisters, and finally* EMILY *begins to sing. The others join, followed by* PATCH *and the whole* ASSEMBLY. *Then* MOULE *and* MRS MOULE *emerge into the street, and begin the walk back to Fordington.*

2.6.3. The High Street, Dorchester. *As the* MOULES *process back through the streets of Dorchester to their home, a hymn is sung, and* CITIZENS *speak a eulogy.*

HYMN. Praise my soul, the King of Heaven;
　　　　To his feet thy tribute bring,
　　　　Ransom'd, heal'd restor'd, forgiven,
　　　　Who like me his praise should sing?
　　　　Praise him! Praise him!
　　　　Praise him! Praise him!
　　　　Praise the everlasting King.

CITIZENS. So what can we say of the man who has borne the brunt of this terrible visitation?

What can we say of him who has been to the bedside of all the victims stricken in his unlucky parish?

Who has watched the plague, and gone with never-tiring step,
and ever-ready consolation,

to soothe those who lay beneath its all-devouring ravishes?

Who has been present in the midst of its greatest miseries,
and with its most wretched victims.

What of him – Henry Moule, the most amiable of vicars?

He is God's servant truly.

Meanwhile the hymn has continued:

HYMN. Fatherlike he tends and spares us;
        Well our feeble frame he knows;
        In his hands he gently bears us,
        Rescues us from all our foes.
        Praise him! Praise him!
        Praise him! Praise him!
        Widely as his mercy flows.

        Angels help us to adore him,
        Ye behold him face to face;
        Sun and moon bow down before him,
        Dwellers all in time and space.
        Praise him! Praise him!
        Praise him! Praise him!
        Praise with us the God of Grace.

And the MOULES *are back home together, clasping each other's
hands tightly.* MRS MOULE *whispers to her husband:*

MRS MOULE. And there was a man, who came from God. And
the same came for a witness, to bear witness to the light. That all
men through him should believe.

Scene Seven

2.7.1. **The Roof of King's College Chapel, Cambridge.** *Dawn.
Brilliant, low light. It is a few years later.* CHARLES MOULE, *in
his academic gown, with* HORACE.

HORACE. The towers of Jerusalem.

CHARLES. I'm sorry?

HORACE. Don't you think? Through the morning mist? The spires of Ely, gleam and glisten, like unto the Towers of Jerusalem?

CHARLES. Yes. Yes, indeed.

HORACE. Now, Charles. This is my privilege. To introduce you to this sight. The vision from the roof of King's, King's College Chapel, at the very break of dawn. You might at least affect to be impressed.

CHARLES. I am impressed.

HORACE. Your right, of course, to witness, as a distinguished fellow of the University. Mine as an undistinguished, undeserved MA.

CHARLES. You are entitled –

HORACE. A mere, honorary honour. Coupled with what I imagine is a more or less unique distinction, to have plucked at *both* our ancient universities.

CHARLES. Look, Horace, are you –

HORACE. Charles. Do you know what I do with my days?

Pause.

CHARLES. You are an Inspector of the Poor Law for the District of East Anglia. You are, if I may say so, Horace, increasingly occasionally an Inspector of the Poor Law for the District of East Anglia.

HORACE. Or, put another way, I visit unions. Workhouses. It is not attractive work, I have to tell you, Charles.

CHARLES. I have no doubt. But nonetheless –

HORACE. Last month. An aborted baby, rammed into a soil-pipe. Another, well, newborn, found strangled on the doorstep. As 'a deadborn baby, sirs, please put it underground'. So is it any wonder that my duties are occasionally – occasional?

CHARLES. It is no wonder. But it is a fault.

HORACE. Aha. A *fault*. Oh, how I hear our father. Ah. A *fault*. The genus Moule. *Flagrante*.

CHARLES *says nothing.*

How is he?

CHARLES. He is well. He has patented a scheme for converting shale to gas, which has engaged his interest.

HORACE. Ah, yes, the schemes. And the contrivances. How go the sales of his earth closet?

CHARLES. Not as well as hoped. But they are used in several prisons. And our cabbages and roses grow in great profusion.

Slight pause. CHARLES *smiles.*

In fact, he preached upon the subject. On the seventh Sunday after Trinity. Drawing his inference from Deuteronomy.

HORACE *smiles.*

HORACE. I see.

Slight pause.

Oh, Charles. Do you know my difficulty? With my father?

CHARLES. No, I do not.

HORACE. It's that I can't believe the truth of everything can be drawn from Deuteronomy. Is actually seared down in that book for ever.

CHARLES. Horace, you know that I believe that what is in that book is for all time.

HORACE. Oh, Charles, I am. So full of fear.

He tries a smile.

Fear and Foreboding.

Pause.

CHARLES. Our brother Handley spoke to me of you.

HORACE. No doubt he too had faults to speak of.

CHARLES. No. He spoke of when he was a child and you and he would walk together through the corn, translating Hesiod. Or you'd draw a plan of ancient Rome with lines of pebbles on the lawn. He said – you were the greatest educator he had ever met.

HORACE (*suddenly angry*). Do not – don't talk to me of waste.

Pause.

My son would be a man. I didn't draw a plan of ancient anything for him.

Pause.

CHARLES. Your son?

HORACE. Or daughter. I don't know.

Slight pause.

Whose mother was my mistress. Who for that 'fault' was packed off half-way round the world.

Pause.

D'you see?

CHARLES. Horace, I'm going down.

HORACE. A moment, and I'll follow you.

CHARLES. I'll wait.

HORACE. A *moment*, Charles.

CHARLES *shrugs and goes.*

From here, you see, in the brilliant light of morning, you can see no workhouses. And yet too bright. Oh, far, oh far too blinding bright to bear.

Lights cut back to MRS MOULE, standing where we left her, but without her husband.

MRS MOULE (*surprised*). Uh, Henry. Henry?

She realises.

Oh, Henry, I can't *see* . . .

Lights back to the roof of King's.

HORACE. For George, Prince George, what have you done.
            You have slain your own beloved son.
            You have cut him down, in the morning sun.

HORACE *throws himself from the roof into the darkness below.*

Scene Eight

2.8.1. **Fordington: The Churchyard and Streets.** *A performance of a* MUMMERS' *play – but this time, as it were, for real: a group of actual* MUMMERS *are performing their play round the houses of Fordington, within sound of the churchyard. The* DEAD MUMMER *lies on the ground, the St George cross lying beside. The* PRESENTER *stands.*

As the scene gets under way, lights come up on HENRY MOULE, *kneeling by the grave of his son* HORACE *in St George's churchyard, and a* WOMAN *standing behind him. It is Christmas time.*

PRESENTER. Is there a doctor to be found
　　　　　All ready near at hand,
　　　　　To cure this dread and deathly wound
　　　　　And make the champion stand.

Enter the DOCTOR.

DOCTOR. I am a doctor.

PRESENTER. Doctor?

DOCTOR. Ay.

PRESENTER. From whence and why?

DOCTOR. From whither of the world around,
　　　　　For why to cure him on the ground.
　　　　　Of the stich, itch and ague, the blight of the lame
　　　　　And for half a pence more, the dead raise up again.

2.8.2 **The Churchyard.** *The* WOMAN *speaks to* MOULE. *It's* SARAH.

SARAH. Well, once again. We overhear a pagan ritual.

MOULE. I'm sorry?

SARAH. Mr Moule. You may not readily remember. I am Sarah Eldridge, from the Dragon Brewery.

MOULE. Oh, yes. And what, may I enquire –

SARAH. Well, let's say, I do feel that in this, season of goodwill, that it do seem appropriate . . .

MOULE. Yes? What?

SARAH. To offer my condolences to you.

Slight pause.

In the tragic loss of your dear son.

Pause.

MOULE (*thickly*). I thank you.

SARAH. A loss that bears comparison, you see, with my loss of my son. But perhaps, as well, with mine of my, dear husband.

MOULE. Mrs Eldridge, I'm not sure –

SARAH. Which loss, I think, that you do term a suicide.

Pause.

MOULE. The balance of my son's mind was disturbed.

SARAH. Both your son and my husband had disturbed their own minds over many years.

MOULE. Mrs Eldridge, what is the purpose of this visitation?

SARAH. Oh, Mr Moule, we share so much. Why not a little understanding?

Pause.

MOULE. So, ma'am. What would you have me understand.

SARAH. Well, maybe, how harsh the burning light of virtue feels. To those whose own virtue burns less bright. To those who stand in shadow.

Pause.

And that while it is indeed a fault to think all strangers immanently good, it is perhaps as grave a one, to think that those we know and try to love are, well – 'beyond reprieve'.

Pause. MOULE *stands and looks at* SARAH.

MOULE. And are you still a brewer, Mrs Eldridge?

SARAH. Well, retired.

MOULE. You will not expect me, ma'am, to grieve at that.

SARAH. Well, no. No more do I. But there are always things, that one is sad to lose.

MOULE. I must confess, that in this case, I can't imagine –

SARAH. There is of all things an old and battered copper set, which I used for boiling hops, back in my first days, to which I am peculiarly attached.

MOULE. A what?

SARAH. A copper. You know, like an ordinary, domestic copper boiler. Larger, naturally . . .

MOULE. You mean, within the brewery –

SARAH. That's right. Though, in fact, the one I'm thinking of has not been used for many years. Not indeed, I think, since 1854.

Slight pause.

September 1854.

Slight pause.

The night when my three daughters, without my permission or consent – and aided and abetted by what I had thought to be four loyal stablehands – loaded it up on the back of my biggest dray and rode it down to Fordington, and set it down, and built a fire, to boil and disinfect the clothing of the dying and the dead, to try and help some strange old parson stop the pestilence from spreading into Dorchester.

Pause. MOULE *looks wild-eyed.*

Uh – Mr Moule?

MOULE. Mrs Eldridge. You said – three?

SARAH. That's right. Emily, and little Sarah. And – and Sophie. Who –

MOULE. The three.

SARAH. I'm sorry?

MOULE. I did not understand. I had been entertaining angels unawares.

SARAH. Oh, I assure you, Mr Moule –

She stops herself.

Well, maybe. In a way.

Pause.

And it do take me some time to appreciate. That until we loose the bonds of strangers, then the cup we raise behind our gates is gall.

But also, that the strangers we must entertain include our own. And the bonds we loose are not just theirs, but ours.

A moment. Then HANDLEY JNR *appears. He is in clerical clothes.*

HANDLEY JNR. Now, father. *Here* you are.

MOULE. Why, Handley. What's the matter?

HANDLEY JNR. Father, it's a young woman, from the back of Ansty. She can't be more than seventeen. And she's come to talk to us of marriage.

MOULE. Then certainly, we have to talk to her.

HANDLEY JNR. And she is obviously –

Conscious of SARAH:

– considerably, far gone.

MOULE. I see. Where is she now?

HANDLEY JNR. She's in the Vicarage. She's reading to mama.

MOULE. Well, that's kind.

HANDLEY JNR. No doubt, in order to ingratiate –

MOULE. No doubt.

Slight pause.

And you're quite right. Her fault is grave. And we must tell her so, in no uncertain terms.

HANDLEY JNR *turns and goes off, back towards church. Perhaps he just hears his father.*

But, maybe. There are even graver.

MOULE *turns to* SARAH.

SARAH. Oh, Mr Moule. St George.

MOULE. I beg your pardon?

SARAH. Your St George. And his true story. Who of course was not a dragon-slayer, but a martyr. Who was told by God he would be killed three times. And after his first martyrdom, his body was cut up and spread about the land. But St Michael the great angel gathered up the pieces, like a harvest, and God made him live again. And sometimes he be called Green George, the dead king who is burnt, and scattered on the frozen earth, to bring it back to life.

For we must remember, must we not, that like trees men have roots and trunks, which thrust up to the sky, but also branches which stretch out to other men, and touch them.

Pause.

For only thus may we divine – from what, strange soil, may green things grow.

2.8.3. **The Mummers.** *Enter the previously* DEAD MUMMER, *holding the George cross flag. He circles* MOULE *and* SARAH.

RESURRECTED MUMMER.
> Oh George, King George, where have I been,
> What strange and wondrous sights I've seen;
> What places there,
> What scenes appear,
> Since I the harrow entered in.
>
> A hundred echoes round me cross
> From hill to hill the voices tossed,
> From high to low
> They singing go
> And not a single word is lost.
>
> Behold on yonder risen ground,
> The Holy City all around,
> Never from wending,
> Never be ending,
> Hark to its eternal sound.

And at first in the distance, but then drawing closer, we hear an old wassailing song, which as it grows brings all the COMPANY *on to the stage – the survivors and the victims, the living and the dead – who first surround and then swallow up* HENRY MOULE *and* SARAH ELDRIDGE, *as, in the end, all voices join together:*

COMPANY. How far have we travelled, how far do we hie
Some good cheer to bring now that Christmas be nigh
And our wassail be made of the good ale and true
'Tis nutmeg and ginger the best we can brew

Our wassail is made of the elderberry bow
And so my good neighbours we drink unto thou
We pray that on earth you'll have plenty in store,
And let us come in for 'tis cold by the door.

Up and down, through all the town
and all around,
so far we been:
Sing wassail sing a-wassail
And call you us in

For we know by the moon that we are not too soon
And we know by the sky that we are not too high
And we know by the stars that we are not too far
And we know by the ground that we are within
sound

Up and down, through all the town
and all around,
how far we been:
Sing wassail sing a-wassail
And call you us in

There's a master and a missus sat down by the fire
While we poor plough boys stand here in the mire
And you pretty maid with your silver-headed pin
Pray open the door and let us come in

So fair maidy so fair lady
with your silver headed pin –
Won't you come to, to your window
And let us come in